INTERSIGHT

ACKNOWLEDGEMENTS

Intersight is made possible through the Fred Wallace Brunkow Fellowship, an endowment by Kathryn Brunkow Sample and Steven B. Sample, former President of the University at Buffalo, State University of New York. The publication of *Intersight* is also made possible through the continued generosity and support of Cannon Design Corporation.

There is no single person or group that is responsible for the publication of *Intersight*. The journal is made possible only through the collaborative efforts of the School's students and faculty. As editor, the Brunkow Fellow represents the larger community of students in the School of Architecture and Planning and it has been a profound honor to serve in that capacity for the past two years.

Upon nomination to the Fellowship in 2004 Dean Brian Carter asked if it would be possible to publish *Intersight* annually. To increase the frequency of the publication, it was crucial to evaluate what *Intersight* would become in the process. This introspection began with a return to the original intentions of Kathryn and Steven Sample upon establishing the Fred Wallace Brunkow Fellowship 17 years ago. The Samples had envisioned that *Intersight* would become "...a folio publication of the best works by students currently enrolled in the School of Architecture and Planning." With that in mind, *Intersight* strives to be a visualization of the school's planning and design pedagogy. Additionally, it presents the events, workshops and distinguished visitors whose lectures and critical commentary have raised the level of discourse and thereby influenced the work of the students represented within.

I wish to express heartfelt thanks to Dean Brian Carter, and Professor Annette LeCuyer for their moral and editorial support these past two years. Many thanks are also due to Ruth Bryant, William McDonnell, Cheryl O'Donnell and Barbara Pattoli for their managerial support. Special thanks to the entire advisory board and our design associates Michele Han, Tsui Ying Ip (Jade) and Clare Smith who collectively have helped raise the bar again this year. Thanks again to our proofreaders Jennifer Oakley and Rachel Stecker. *Intersight* could not be sustained without quality content, and we are indebted to all the students and faculty of the school for your valuable contributions and collaboration.

Finally, a special dedication to Kirsten, for being my steadfast partner through the process and to the two little ladies who fill our home with effervescent joy.

William C. Helm II
2004-2006 Fred Wallace Brunkow Fellow

INTERSIGHT v9.06

CONTENTS

FOREWORD

'The Buffalo Effort' was acknowledged by *Progressive Architecture* as a plan 'to change totally a pattern of education'. Embracing the vision of a school focused on a broad definition of design, an enthusiasm for material, craft and open, day-lit spaces which recall the workshops that characterize our city and the spirit of modernism, it is a plan that we are advancing.

Our school epitomizes the creative processes of making plans and realizing architecture – processes that are raw and messy yet founded in deep, diverse agendas of research and close collaborations which demand the inspiration of hand, eye and mind.

This annual publication provides a new glimpse of that place and of the work being done there. It is work by students and faculty busy in buildings on the Main Street of a city steeped in good architecture and inspired civic planning. It is work by many different people, work created out of discussion and debate, by cutting and casting, through the virtual space of the screen and intense physical labor. It is work that records the most recent efforts in Buffalo to change, define and construct patterns for the education of architects, regional planners and city designers.

Brian Carter
Professor and Dean.

DAN CHORLEY, STEWART GOEHRINGER

STUMP
Freshmen Studio at Griffis Sculpture Park

FRANK FANTAUZZI
MICHAEL ZEBROWSKI

TEACHING ASSISTANTS
Seth Amman
Justin Allen
Joe Carline
Anne Elrod
Dan Gallagher
Dave Goldstein
John Scanlan
Matt Zinski

STUDENTS
Shannon Brennan
Dan Chorley
Michael Cross
Joe Diperna
Shawn Faulkner
Lauren Giamundo
Stewart Goehringer
David Johnson
Nicole Lamie
Dan Mannino
Emily Oare
Brian Podleski
Rob Przybysz
Vail Rooney
Chris Scherer
Chris Sclafani
Amy Sekol
Dan Setnikar
Joe Shand
Keith Short
Saki Yoshimura
Matt Zych

Stump is a project executed in a wooded area of Griffis Sculpture Park in Ashford Hollow, New York, during Spring 2005. It involves 46 site-specific interventions in existing tree stumps, utilizing cutting and casting processes. These projects intervene in nature's cycle of life and death. They are optimistic and architectural because they attempt permanence. They were made by architecture students working in teams at the end of their first year.

DAVID JOHNSON, EMILY OARE

DAN MANNINO, CHRIS SCHERER

NICOLE LAMIE, MATT ZYCH

MICHAEL CROSS, CHRIS SCLAFANI

SHANNON BRENNAN, ROB PRZYBYSZ

DESIGN STUDIO 102 . SPRING 2005

AMY SEKOL, JOE SHAND

DAN CHORLEY, STEWART GOEHRINGER

SHAWN FAULKNER, DAN SETNIKAR

JOE DIPERNA, KEITH SHORT

LAUREN GIAMUNDO, VAIL ROONEY

BRIAN PODLESKI, SAKI YOSHIMURA

DESIGN STUDIO 102 . SPRING 2005

KURTIS LANNING

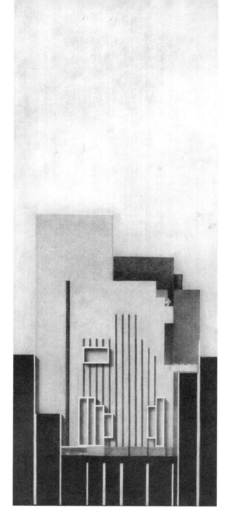

SZE WAN (SHARON) LI

LAUREN INSALACO

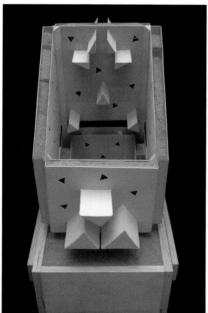

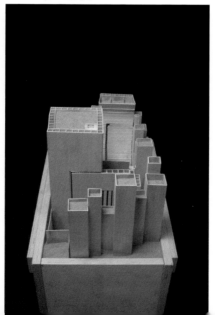

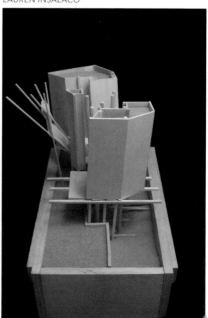

ELEMENTAL HOUSE

"The materiality of my body both coincides with and struggles with the materiality of space."
Bernard Tschumi

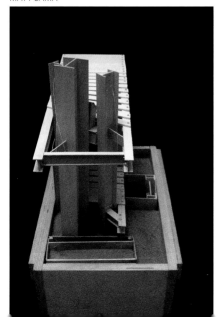

MATT SAMA

BETH TAUKE
MICHAEL ZEBROWSKI

TEACHING ASSISTANTS
Seth Amman
Erina Ardianto
Nick Bruscia
Erin Cox
David Goldstein
Peter Heller
Kevin Moran
Jen Oakley
John Scanlan
James Sternick

STUDENTS
Jennifer Frelock
Matt Sama
Jian Feng You
Aaron Tarnowski
Kurtis Lanning
Takako Yoshikuni
Sze Wan (Sharon) Li
Lauren Insalaco
Stergios Zissis

The body and the ground are two insistent realities that both limit and open the possibilities of spatial experience. They are the starting points for this beginning architectural exploration; the body is the instrument that displaces ground and materials to shape space for its own occupation.

Although the body that inhabits a house is often not visible, its patterns and vestiges can be detected through material and structural formulation, which "generate and register a 'fit' between material conditions and the conditions of the occupant."
The Elemental House contains spaces for the human body in its basic positions (standing, sitting, and lying) and extends ideas about these postures into basic life functions. It is a recording device on several levels: first, it registers the body through its making; second, it indexes the body through proportional and formal relationships; and third, it acknowledges the body in space and time through the manipulation of the ground plane.

"Three moments in the successive transformation of bodily projection seem especially important for contemporary theorists: these might be described concisely as 1) the notion that building is a body of some kind; 2) the idea that the building embodies states of the body or, more importantly, states of mind based on bodily sensation; and 3) the sense that the environment as a whole is endowed with bodily or at least organic characteristics."
Anthony Vidler

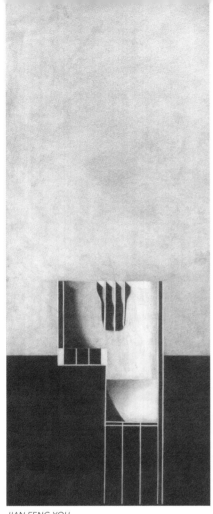

JIAN FENG YOU

JENNIFER FRELOCK

AARON TARNOWSKI

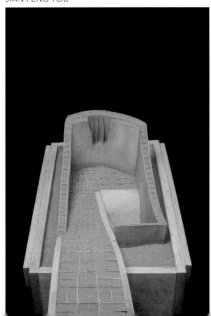

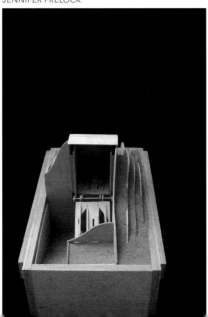

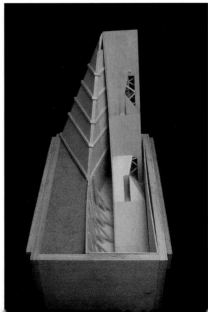

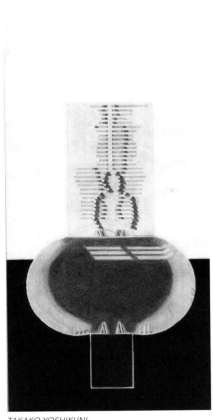

TAKAKO YOSHIKUNI

STERGIOS ZISSIS

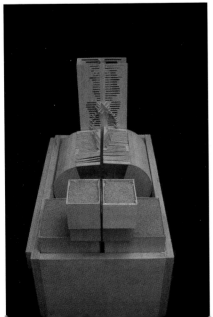

The project moves the body beyond 'object' by establishing it as part of a system of interdependent processes that include the 'figure' as both figure and ground and the 'ground' as both figure and ground. The house evolves as a result of digging in sand—on the one hand, an act of survival, and the other, of childhood pleasure--and building retaining structures that reference body postures to support the displaced sand.

The exploration was structured as a series of studies that focused on notions of 'house' as that which is comprised of body conditions, materials, space, time, and structure situated in a basic domestic program:

Posture models
Students designed constructions for three postures: standing, lying, and sitting. Each of these spaces was made by folding/scoring a single manila folder.

Site displacement
Students made a 10" x 20" x 10" plywood box, and filled it with sand. They displaced 500 cubic inches of sand above the ground plane to develop a site for the three spaces for standing, lying, and sitting.

Hybrid
Students developed a logic for merging the posture models with the retaining conditions into a single hybrid model that was integrated into the site.

Drawings
Students used section and paraline drawings to generate and analyze the assembly, lighting, circulation, structure, and embodiment of the Elemental House.

Through this project students studied ground, materials, and space as extensions of the human body. They explored the spatial relationships between the subject and object; ways that figure/ground shifts influence perception; and how the shape of space/material affects experiences, in particular, architectural experiences.

DESIGN STUDIO 101 . FALL 2005

BURAK PEKOGLU, SHAWN FAULKNER

CONSTRUCTING CONSTRUCTIVIST CONSTRUCTIONS

The sophomore year has been constructed around the analysis of historical precedents and their transformation into new architecture. The work of the Fall 2005 semester was devoted to explorations of selected projects of the Russian Constructivists.

SHADI NAZARIAN
TORBEN BERNS
DANIEL GALLAGHER
DENNIS MAHER
CHRIS ROMANO
MATT ZINSKI

Matt Bull
Shannon Brennan
Joseph Diperna
Shawn Faulkner
Josh Gardner
Aaron Henderson
Pavel Fesyuk
Jonathan Kin Cho Ma
Phil Krull
Burak Pekoglu
Rafael Ramirez
Ciara Seymour
Keerati Smathrithayavech
Gary Williams

TIMELINE DRAWING
Students began the semester by conducting analyses of Vladimir Tatlin's Monument to the Third International. They were asked to construct a drawing which communicated critical moments in the generative process of the tower: to exhibit its temporal program and choreography, to give appearance to the forces implied within it, and to expose the traces of the structural and programmatic forces in action in order to to construct a record of the performative structure.

PAINTINGS BY MALEVICH
Subsequently, students were exposed to the Suprematist paintings of Malevich. They were asked to consider states of balance/imbalance, stability/instability, tension/compression, and motion/rest. Each work was presented as "a record of a process frozen instantaneously or within a limited duration in time." Each was emphasized as "merely a fragment of a sequence, which alludes to something before and after that moment or duration...becoming... not fixed." Students were responsible for producing a set of mechanical models and drawings that proposed and tested the sequence/progression to which each painting might belong.

TECTONIC LANDSCAPE
Discussions and lectures about Constructivism revealed the interdependence of formal/spatial languages and social ideology. In the final phase of the semester, students were asked to develop a social program (generically termed "garden") which was born out of their analytical studies. Each student was required to synthesize key concepts in the design of an operable cantilever construction. The site for the cantilever was a concrete masonry wall four units high which was built as a part of the studio. In addition to performing at the scale of the wall, the construction was to simultaneously address its representational potential as an idealized, tectonic landscape.

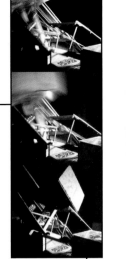
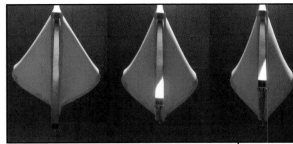

CIARA SEYMOUR designed a constantly changing tectonic garden, drawing different experiences as a counterweight's movement farther from the fulcrum point causes a concrete block to dump its contents (rocks formerly in the wall) onto an affixed skin of spandex. When the counterweight is moved closer to the fulcrum the system moves back and the rocks are dumped back into the block creating a constantly changing tectonic garden.

SHANNON BRENNAN designed her garden to make visible the forces of tension, compression and gravity. The individual moving through the cantilevered structure becomes the weight necessary to activate these forces and set in motion a unique spatial experience as the space transforms around them.

NAZARIAN STUDIO

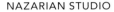

AARON HENDERSON; As the occupancy of the center plane increases and it begins to sink, the outer planes will rise. This upward movement is controlled by elements inside the wall, causing the outer planes to rotate on an axis perpendicular to the wall, into a purely vertical, depopulated state.

MATT BULL, GARY WILLIAMS; The extrusion of Malevich into Crosby room 5 intensified the spatial experience of the painting as geometric volumes were held in space in tension, and masks created moving shadows the sunlight in the room.

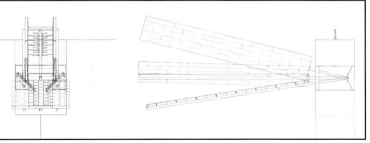

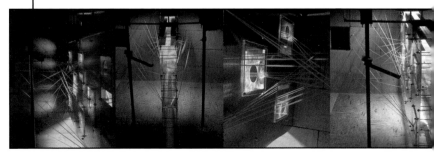

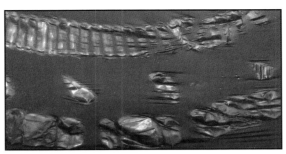

TIMELINE: CIARA SEYMOUR, SHANNON BRENNAN produced a timeline document that illustrates the program of Tatlin's monument by wrapping spandex tightly around an operating scaled reproduction of the monument. As the three solids rotated at their respective speeds they left traces of their contact in specific moments in time.

GALLAGHER STUDIO

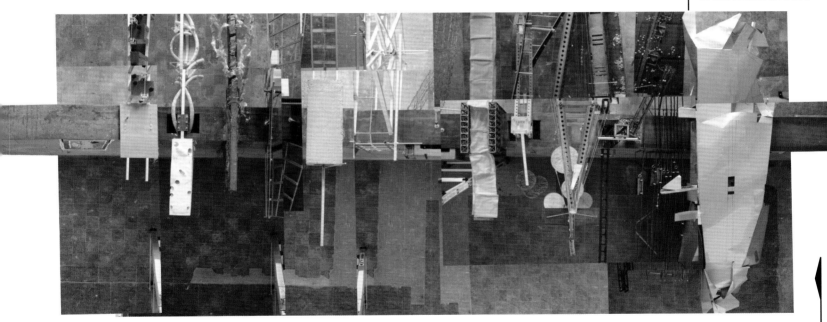

The constructivist garden began as the space between two volumetric planes cantilevered off the wall, following the grid previously applied to Crosby room 5, produced masks through which a tuning apparatus weaves infrastructural elements between volumes.

DESIGN STUDIO 201 . FALL 2005

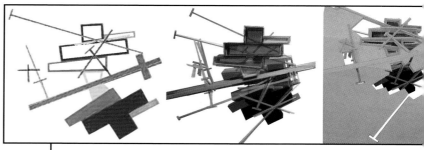

SHAWN FAULKNER, JOSEPH DIPERNA; Volumetric and linear forces bring about breakdown and separation. Rotational forces enhance separation through the grid structure.

MAHER STUDIO

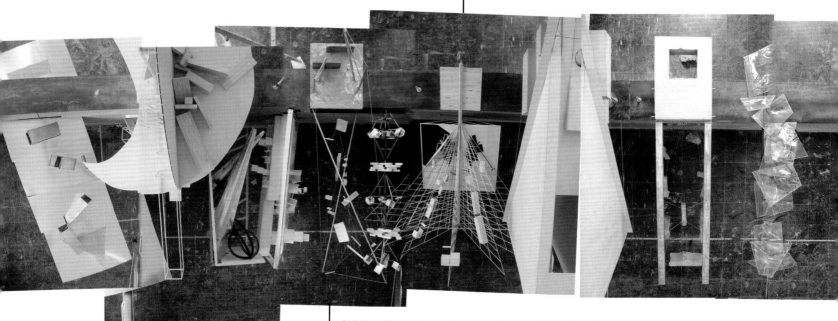

BURAK PEKOGLU; The cantilever is positioned at an ideal balance. Two arms attached to the wall are controlled by two heavy masses, the governing body of the system. The ideal position relies upon the weights, one moving up as the other moves down. A centripetal axis extends on a trajectory. Lighter objects move faster, leaving heavy ones behind.

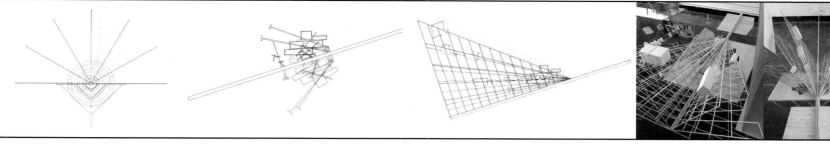

The new garden of forces impose planar, linear and volumetric entities to create a distinct spatial order Within the garden is a separation of a structured public and isolated private areas.

ZINSKI STUDIO

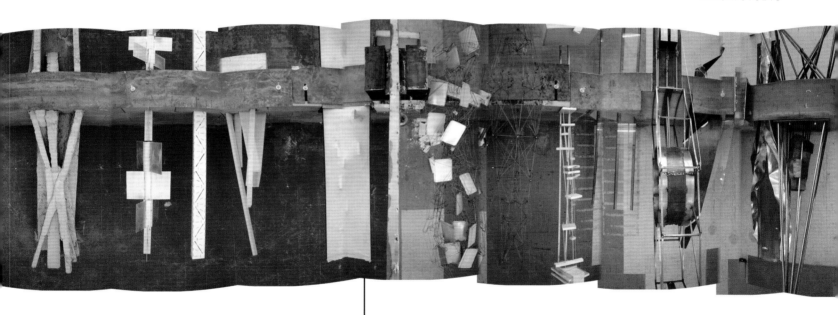

TECTONIC LANDSCAPE: PAVEL FESYUK

DESIGN STUDIO 201 . FALL 2005

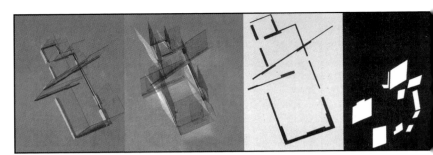

JOSH GARDNER; Two eight foot steel tubes are cantilevered off the wall and utilizing a fulcrum detail to maintain stability. Each linear tube suspends transparent volumes of varying weight that explore the overlap of public and private.

RAFAEL RAMIREZ; One-sixteenth inch aluminum plate was sheared into a puzzle of triangular shapes and bolted together forming faceted surface. This surface was manipulated to different degrees of intensity to represent a smooth transition between public to private spaces.

ROMANO STUDIO

PHIL KRULL; A folded sheet of steel plate explored the relationship between public and private space as it moved through the concrete masonry wall.

TIMELINE CONSTRUCT: KEERATI SMATHRITHAYAVECH, JONATHAN KIN CHO MA

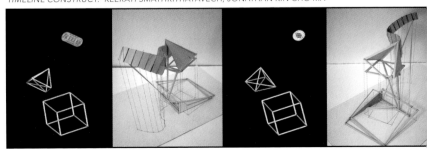

JONATHAN KIN CHO MA; Malevich's "Suprematism 1918" is used to create a "shadow projection" where a hypothetical projection of a moving light source would produce the original Malevich painting. A device is then created which would allow and actualize this relation of light and shadow. The project results from the projection of both cast shadow and refracted light produced by the device. The volume of space created between these two projections forms the basis of the proposal.

BERNS STUDIO

KEERATI SMATHRITHAYAVECH; The cantilever is a hinging and folding the structure. An opened cantilevere folds on itself until it is no longer cantilevered. Cast concrete shapes from the painting are placed onto the structure causing it to fold back into the wall.

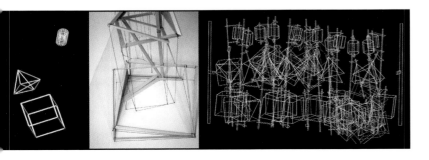

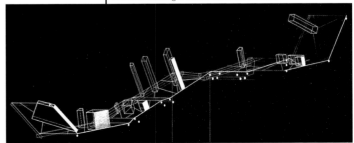

SITUATION AND CONTEXT

LAURA GAROFALO
TORBEN BERNS
KEVIN CONNERS
KAREN TASHJIAN

James Brucz
Gerardo Ciprian
Omar Hakeem
Timothy Hoskins
Matthew Hume
Chris Mackowiak
Andrew Petrinec
Nicole Scharlau
Kimberly Suczynski

The Junior Studio sought to develop the ability to generate architectural design based on a deeper and more qualitative understanding of context. Based on the premise that we inhabit a world of ideas and events as much as one of physicality, the student is asked to reconcile a deeper understanding of context as both the literal and figurative space one moves through. Students were asked to evaluate both the possibilities, and drawbacks of focusing on physical and cultural situations of place. Thus, context was considered in its physicality but with the primary focus on the contemporaneous events that form the mental environment we inhabit. Construction and organization of spaces as well as the appearance and behaviors associated with specific activities were considered. These were explored to generate programmatic and formal solutions.

These topics were engaged through two building projects. The first project took place on the sites of three iconic houses of the 20th century. This analytical project began by literally reading the physical context. Three types of "texts" were read to understand "site" conditions: architectural drawings of the houses, texts written by their architects, and critical or historical texts about the work. Students examined the houses, the ideas that generated them, as well as present critical responses to them. The results from investigations into these issues were imbued in the design of a Visitor Center/Book Shop for one of the houses. The work was done in teams with the final presentation taking a competition format.

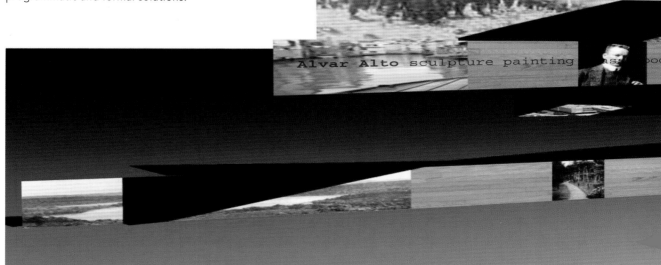

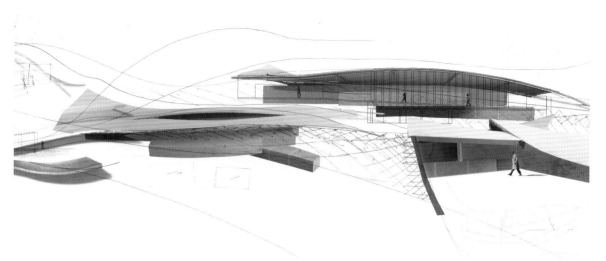

OMAR HAKEEM, TIMOTHY HOSKINS, MATTHEW HUME (ABOVE & BELOW)

The second project explored our contemporary context through a Media Arts Archive adjacent to an existing civic institution. Students were asked to formulate a program as well as a formal response for the project by considering the relationship of content to media both at the level of what they were proposing as well as how they were proposing it. Thus the issue of context demanded both an understanding of the mode of architectural thinking and representation as well its impact on the organization, structure and appearance of the project.

Students were asked to explore the relationship of media with its users. Beginning with visual media, the students formulated a set of rules based on the subject's engagement with that being viewed, location, view and access. This was developed into a wider proposal regarding different types of media. The facility had the option of being joined to the existing institution (a museum) or remain a discrete structure surrounded by the museum. The new proposal was to function as an archival research facility as well as support recreational activities.

OMAR HAKEEM
TIMOTHY HOSKINS
MATTHEW HUME

The perspectives of a certain time and that of the architect Alvar Aalto have forever laminated an experience for our very own perceptions. We are interested in the literal interpretation of this action. The program of the building has been buried under what appears to be a lamination of the ground plane. Giving thought to one's perceptions of the site and its architecture, we wanted to subtly inform the design of the visitor center using this method. Movement through the program, the experience of the ground plane, accessibility, the introduction of its users to a certain context, and its subtle interactions of hold prescience among the design issues of the Villa Mairea visitor center.

The perspectives of Alvar Aalto's time and methods has forever informed the site and architecture of Villa Mairea. It has laminated a particular experience for our own perspectives.

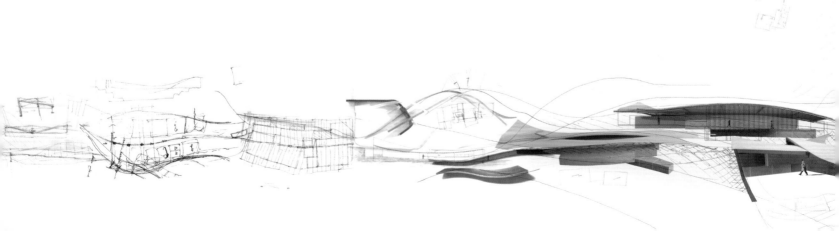

ANDREW PETRINEC
GERARDO CIPRIAN
JAMES BRUCZ

In the Farnsworth House volume is no more, disappeared from mass in an endless bound tectonic frame where moments are made. The technological expression exists between "the flux of tension and gravitational force" of nature. This architectural innovation is housed within an environment, which allows one to step aside from the world only to remain within a culturally universal autonomous context. The grid is established, extending its network of lines subtly into the materials, which epitomizes the linear structure of the edged surface. the site becomes consumed with this lined pattern, fusing rigidity with organic impurity thus establishing a model for a hybrid terrain.

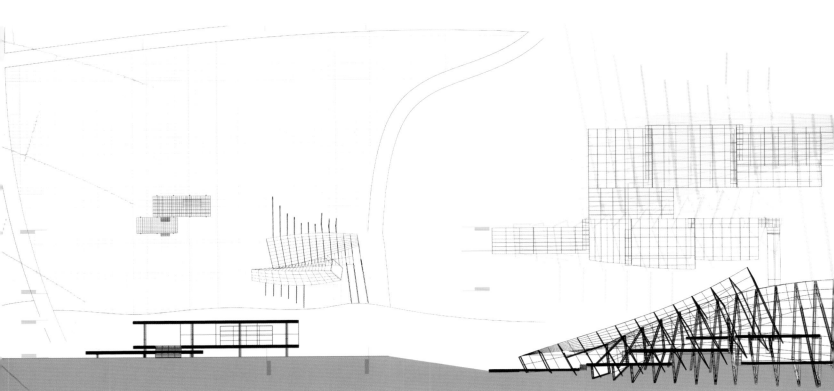

26

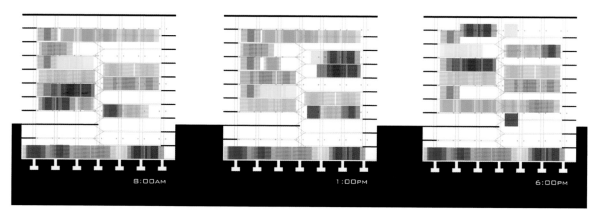

8:00AM   1:00PM   6:00PM

CHRIS MACKOWIAK

The facades of this facility are comprised of large kinetic screens responsive to light values. The screen's deformation is directly proportional to pixel light values of an image with white and black as the two opposite extreme conditions. These screens are receptive of both stills and live media.

To create the most efficient space for archival storage, the computer was reintroduced as a model. Fits of memory can be arranged and rearranged on a hard drive to perform certain tasks with greater ease. Treating program as memory, each interior space was broken down into a 10 x 10 x 10 module which interacts with a structural grid system such that each module can be moved anywhere in the x, y, and z direction. These modules can engage one another to form larger spaces or function as singular units. The building can be programmatically defragmented to maximize efficiency for a certain task or time of day.

NICOLE SCHARLAU

Through examination and experimentation, media develops new meanings, appearing not only as material, but interface, structure, form, subject, and object. Conjunctively, the fold is examined as a mechanism for the production of form and program. The fold and the media come together in an exercise, with each material medium (wood, metal) assigned an "activity medium" (human occupation, technology/image occupation). The resulting space encourages people to experience media in the easy, recreational way that is most common, while at the same time re-examining their relationships and interactions with these same types and manifestations of the media.

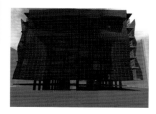

CHRIS MACKOWIAK

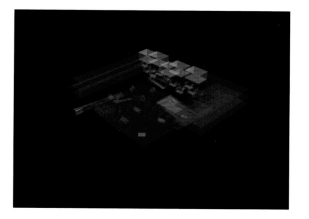

NICOLE SCHARLAU

KIMBERLY SUCZYNSKI

As an addition to the Royal Ontario Museum in Toronto this facility is only accessible through an underground tunnel attached to the existing building. Controlled entry emphasizes the power of the medium of light whilst allowing the building to remain a pristine object in the landscape.

KIMBERLY SUCZYNSKI

TACTICAL URBANISM

ANNETTE LECUYER
HIRO HATA
BRAD WALES
PETER YEADON

Christopher Mackowiak
James Brucz
Nathan Alois
Omar Hakeem
Scott Rhodhamel
Matt Hume
Chul Min Park
Steven Peet

American cities have been profoundly affected by the automobile and the government subsidized construction of the Interstate Highway system after World War II, which created new mobility that enabled people to escape from the city to more dispersed patterns of settlement. Suburbs were advocated as safe havens, in particular for women and children. In 1985, in *Crabgrass Frontier: The Suburbanization of the United States*, historian Kenneth Jackson wrote,

In *S, M, L, XL*, Rem Koolhaas argues, "If there is to be a "new urbanism" it will not be based on the twin fantasies of order and omnipotence; it will be the staging of uncertainty; it will no longer be concerned with the arrangement of more or less permanent objects but with the irrigation of territories with potential;...it will no longer be about...the imposition of limits, but about expanding notions, denying boundaries, discovering unnameable hybrids...

"Pure and unfettered and bathed by sunlight and fresh air, [commuter retreats] offered the exciting prospect that disorder, prostitution, and mayhem could be kept at a distance, far way in the festering metropolis."

The consequent depopulation of cities is not a uniquely American problem. Rem Koolhaas points out in recent research published in *Wired* that many cities in the developed world are stagnant or in decline. In contrast, he observes that cities in the developing world are growing rapidly. Considering the balance, Koolhaas predicts an overall gain so that, by the end of this decade, half of the world's population will live in cities. However, all countries do not conform to Koolhaas' assumptions, and Canada is an important exception. While obviously in a developed country, Canadian cities are booming. Nearly 78 % of Canadians presently live in metropolitan areas, far in excess of Koolhaas' projected worldwide average. Toronto, growing at the rate of 100,000 new residents per year, provides a vibrant laboratory for the study of urban life, both existing and projected.

We were making sand castles. Now we swim in the sea that swept them away."

Cities are arguably the richest, most complex artifact of human culture. For thousands of years, man has both imagined Utopian cities and built real cities. In order to survive, the vision and the reality have had to adapt and change in response to social, economic and political conditions. The cultural milieu that produced walled cities in the past contrasts markedly with the effect of the digital environment on the metropolis. Instead of having to huddle together for safety and for work, the world is more open and interconnected, and people can live and work anywhere. In order for cities to survive and thrive, people now need to be drawn to them for other reasons.

CHUL MIN PARK

CHUL MIN PARK

The public component of this scheme is a film school, a choice that shaped the concept of projection. The film school is located on King Street, in the heart of Toronto's growing theater/film district. Residential units are planned in three towers arrayed along Mercer Street on the south side of the site. This massing creates apertures between the towers that allow sunlight to be 'projected' into the raised film plaza in the middle of the site. Each residential unit has three window orientations including south, north, and either east or west. Living rooms and terraces face the film plaza to enjoy views of proposed film projections onto other building faces. South light is brought into each living room through a slit-like aperture in either the east or west facade. The film plaza is entered via broad flights of stairs from any of the three surrounding streets. The film school has three indoor theaters, a plaza-level amphitheater and eight building surfaces for projection.

During this semester, the 'festering metropolis' was investigated as a territory of potential. The semester focused on the design of a mixed use scheme on King Street in Toronto comprised of housing together with public or semi-public functions developed by individual students to 'charge' the conceptual strategy of their schemes. The task was to think tactically about the potential of the city, to take risks in exploring a speculative position about urban living, and to test this position at the scale of the city, the building and its detail.

JAMES BRUCZ

An in-between realm mediates between the public space of the city and private housing. The scheme becomes permeable, allowing the public to penetrate "dissolved barriers" and flow through the site. To create overall unity, slenderness, and permeability, the structural frame is made of square steel columns filled with reinforced concrete for fireproofing. With exposed structure providing visual coherence and rhythm, glazed cladding intensifies the permeable character of the scheme.

NATHAN ALOIS

This city within the city is derived from a unit concept that, like Escher's drawings, defies gravitational orientation. Two labyrinthine dwellings are tightly interlocked and accessed via winding exterior stairs, yet their individuality and privacy are maintained. Mid-rise blocks define a precise edge along Spadina Avenue and buffer the low-rise cluster behind. Courtyards and roof gardens provide private outdoor spaces for the units. This mat development covers the site, resisting the desire of the high-rise condo culture that is currently popular in Toronto.

JAMES BRUCZ

JAMES BRUCZ

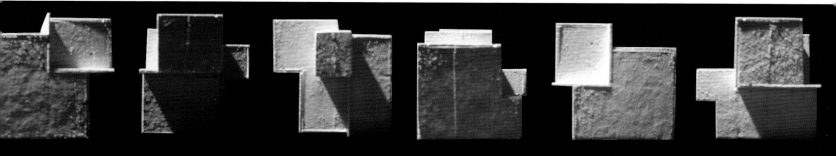

NATHAN ALOIS

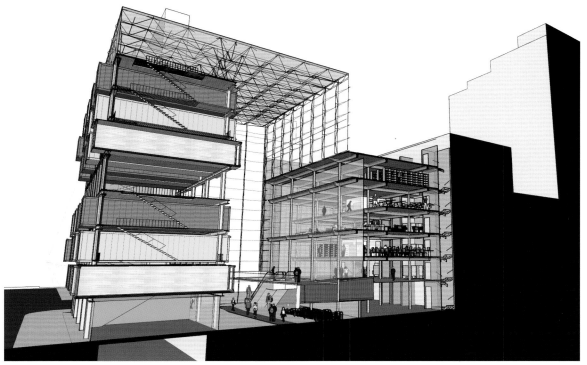

OMAR HAKEEM

OMAR HAKEEM

Custom designed prefabricated modular residential units provide high quality dwellings that are inexpensive to mass produce and easy to assemble. By substantially reducing the suggested area of each dwelling, private space on the site is compacted, allowing both for higher population density and a substantial ground level public space. The scheme includes a community center and three decks of shared semi-public space for occupants.

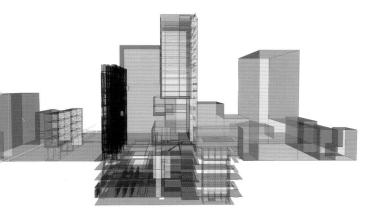

SCOTT RHODHAMEL

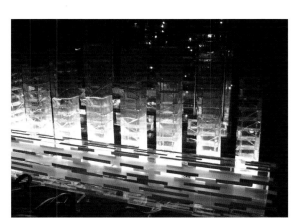

SCOTT RHODHAMEL

Focusing on the concept of movement, a horizontal bar hovers above the busy streetscape, registering the flow of trams and traffic. Towers filter between city and site, street and plinth, sound and calm, buffering the residential slab building that provides the backdrop to the site.

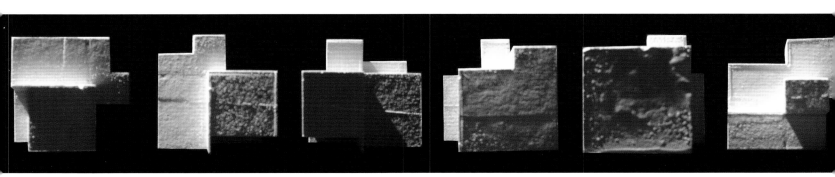

32

MATT HUME

The concept of transition works at many levels. The movement of people is carefully considered between public and private domains, from street to lobby to skip-stop communal terraces, and finally to units. In the commercial program, there is a modulated spatial transition from open streets to a public semi-enclosed market and finally to a bar. Within each unit, there is a multi-level transition between the more public rooms and bedroom areas.

CHRISTOPHER MACKOWIAK

Recent advances in materials science offer exciting opportunities for developing new architectural paradigms. This scheme considers the application of two innovative materials, electro-active polymers and synthetic resilin, in the formation of smart, responsive environments. Resilin is a springy molecule that has been synthesized by biochemists and is significantly more resilient than rubber. It will not lose its elasticity, even when it is repeatedly stretched. Analogous to muscles, electro-active polymers will deform in predictable ways when a current is applied to the material. Both are parlayed into an architecture of animality, where dermatoid membranes sense and respond to activities in the individual residential units and squash courts located across a kinetic atrium. The end result is an affected modulation of sounds emanating from the performance space at the bottom of the crevasse.

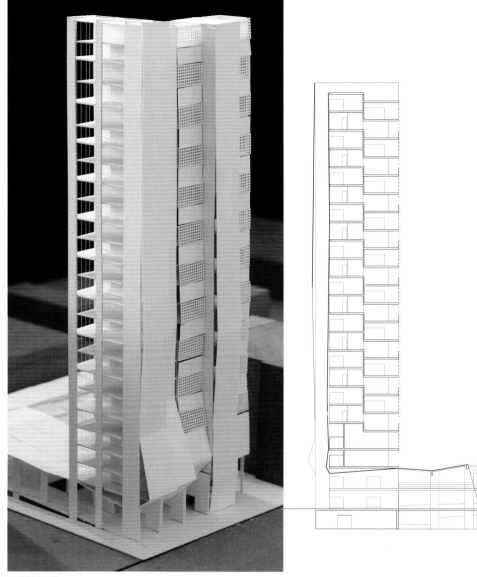

MATT HUME

CHRISTOPHER MACKOWIAK

STEVEN PEET

Climate change, waste, and energy are three significant issues that contemporary architects can no longer ignore. This project examines two aspects of sustainable architecture, the conversion of biowaste to energy and passive solar systems. Beginning with a careful analysis of the site, the form of the edifice was configured to accommodate a complex housing program while ensuring its mass did not cast shadows on neighboring buildings. The residential units are principally oriented to receive east and west exposure to the sun. Each unit has a double exterior glazing system that can modulate heat loss and gain. In summer, the outer layer would be open and the inner layer closed to provide a shaded balcony. In winter, the outer layer would be closed, allowing heat to build up in the enclosed balcony. At the north end of the site, a biomass system turns neighborhood waste into energy for the building.

STEVEN PEET

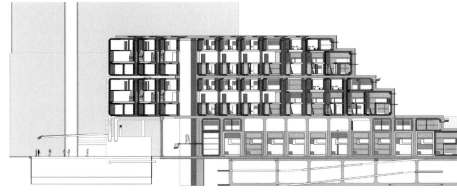

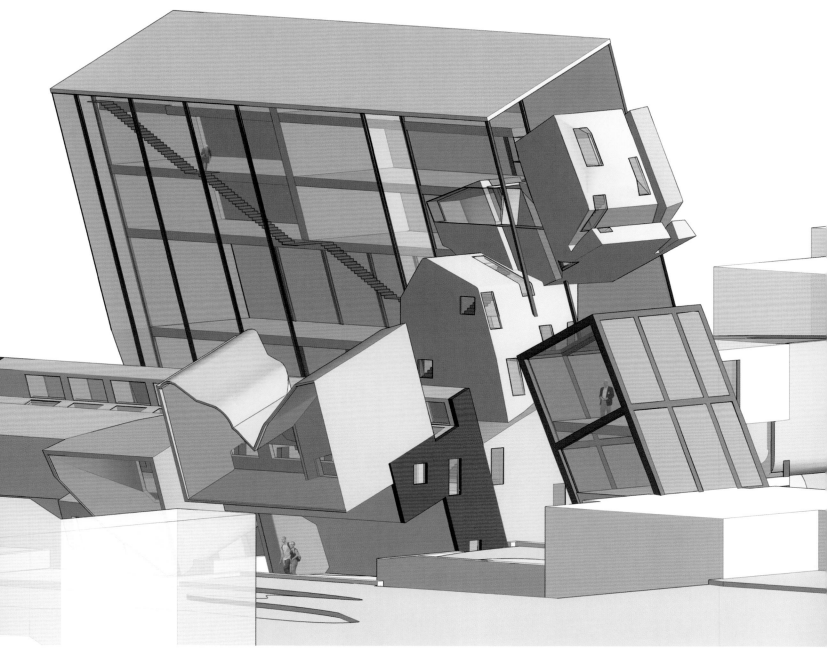

JUSTIN DEGROFF

This project explores the methodology used by Peter Eisenmen to create autonomous architecture though the superimposition of precedent architectural diagrams and existing site conditions. Two drawings, one made up of superimposed plans by Bernini and Schwartz - Silver, and another made up of sections by Holl and Sorkin are created, then further manipulated by imposing a sixteen square grid onto both of them. Each grid is suggestive of the drawing's own symmetries. The gridded drawings are placed onto the site at different scales, fractally overlapping each other and site information. Generic, unfolded, six-sided box patterns are developed in the grids. When the box patterns are folded up, they bring all the site information as well as the original superimposed drawing information into a three-dimensional matrix.

TRACE

"Vestige or mark remaining and indicating the former presence, existence, or action of something, or of a former event or condition."

"The ground-plan of a work."

JEAN LA MARCHE

Justin DeGroff
Sylvia Feng
Peter McCarthy
Ryan Morrissey

This studio explored the ways in which architecture remembers certain acts and how it registers the traces of desire, thought, and value.
The studio began with the proposition that the inherited processes of generating architecture, especially the dictum that form follows function, are not the only means. These and other conventions have been challenged in recent theoretical and practical circles. Alternative possibilities and processes exist that can engage new conjunctions of spaces, materials, constructions, and structures that open up new ways of imagining and producing architecture. The studio explored these possibilities by examining and testing various techniques that have recently held prominence in design such as collage, superposition, palimpsest, erasure, folding, and rotation.

In support of this proposition, students were introduced to some of the work of Peter Eisenman (Cities of Artificial Excavation) and Bernard Tschumi (Architecture and Disjunction). They closely examined Eisenman's process of excavation for the California State University project and Tschumi's ideas and processes used to generate the Parc de la Villette. Initial exercises required that students superpose plans and sections from at least two different buildings on a thick backing, primarily using foamcore. After selecting the buildings, students were asked to literally "excavate", to cut and carve them and, in the process, to register the ideas that were guiding their choices.

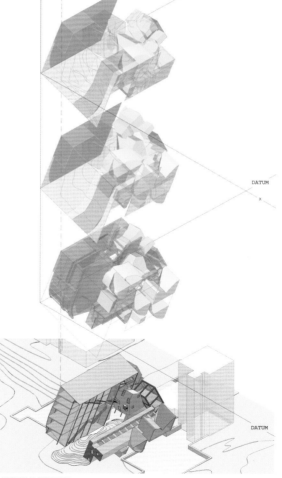

JUSTIN DEGROFF

DESIGN STUDIO 402 . SPRING 2005

The logic and rules that students individually established during these exercises formed the basis for their subsequent phases of the project. Students were asked to find a site, to superpose their excavations over it, and to develop three-dimensional interpretations of the superposed plan/section excavations. As they explored these issues, students developed programs that the work and the site suggested. Their final projects revealed traces of the processes and concepts students used in developing and refining their work.

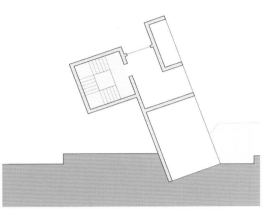

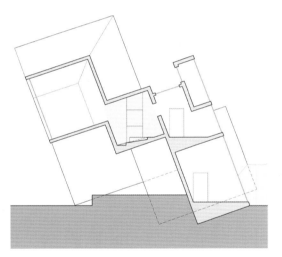

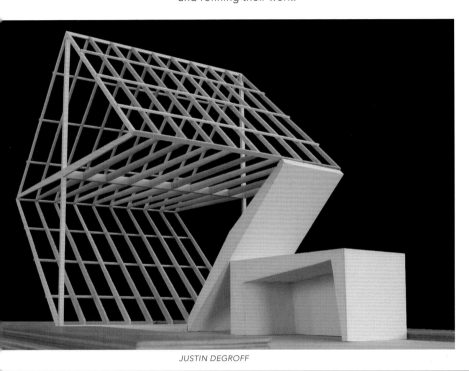

JUSTIN DEGROFF

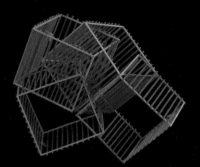
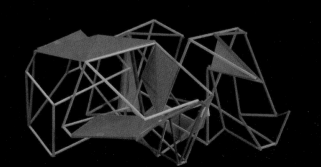

SYLVIA FENG

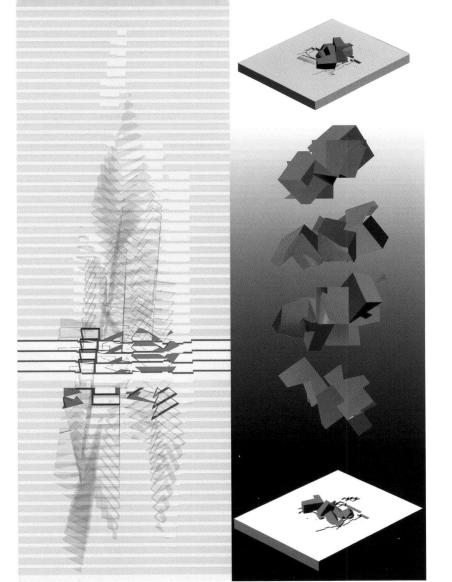

SYLVIA FENG

SYLVIA FENG

The first excavation overlays the plan of St. Peter's Basilica and a synagogue designed by Moshe Safdie for a site in Jerusalem. By superposing the two plans, four significant points of union emerge. The four columns within St. Peters' main dome fall into the column grid of the synagogue. There are two major orthogonal axes that relate to both plans, the true north south line, and the skewed part of the synagogue plan that aligns to the street on the site. Each layer is rotated and the axes and four overlapping squares are carved out of each piece, documenting their migration from layer to layer.

The site selected for the location of a building was on University at Buffalo's South Campus. Four existing metal buildings were manipulated in the same way as the plans in the first exercise, resulting in an excavated site for a new building.

The building volume was derived from the squares in the first exercise. Two copies of the selected clusters of squares were modeled and intersected. The intersecting mass within the connecting cubes was removed and a residual volume resulted. The volume was rotated, placed into the excavated site, and sectioned into ten foot strips to study the interior conditions of the volumes.

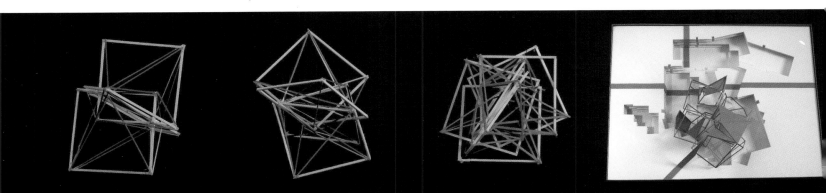

38

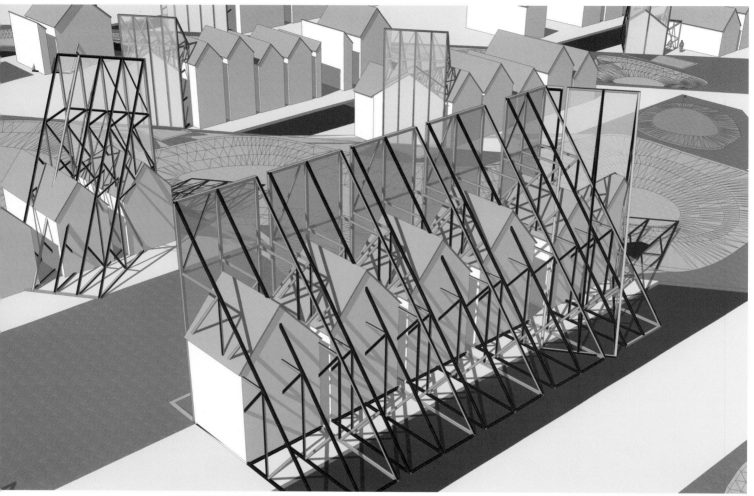

PETER MCCARTHY, RYAN MORRISSEY

Stemming from a study of excavation, the cross-sectional limits of depth were explored rigorously throughout various cuts and removals of project space. The result of these explorations was curiously driven toward six slices; each of which presented individuality within sectional form. Every unique piece, having character relating closely to the original whole, was subsequently applied to a series of South Buffalo residential city blocks. The chosen site highlighted qualities similar to the initial topographical study, revolving around six separate units, each individual in nature, while always preserving a strong relationship to the whole.

As the information discovered in the initial focus was applied to actual landscape, the objectivity of severe sectional intrusion became the focus. Simple two story residential town houses were exposed to a violent introduction of new space. This exposure drove the work toward harnessing the fresh persona of the altered constructs. The houses independently received a new and exciting reconstruction, involving various levels of material removal. This elimination of physical obstruction provided long and thin pathways across the site in a non-orthographic manner. The paths were volatile at this state and were in need of additional barriers for physical stability. Due to the nature of the alley-like forms, golf was chosen to further program the area. The manner in which the houses were reconfigured revolved around the level of protection the nature of golf required. Shielding for the houses was required at various heights and widths. As a result, this foreign application of the sport severely influenced the game itself. The intimate, yet also intimidating surroundings drove the game from a sport of carefully directed unobstructed flight, to an impact driven game of banks and deflection. A new series of actions which represent the verticality and public nature of urban living arose through the altered state of the "urban links."

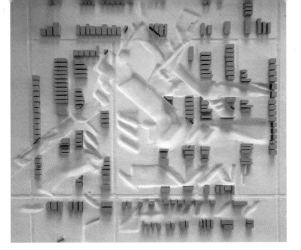

PETER MCCARTHY, RYAN MORRISSEY

KINETIC STRUCTURES

SHAHIN VASSIGH

Farnaz Bakhshi
Golnaz Bakhshi
Nicholas Bruscia
Peter McCarthy
James Teese

Recent technological innovation has created many new possibilities for the design and utilization of kinetic structures. Kinetic architecture has traditionally been conceived as expandable, foldable, and/or portable structures, but with the advent of computing technology, new kinetic architecture is being developed using intelligent systems, which change in response to environmental conditions or human interaction.   Innovators in the field are seeking to develop buildings and building components which by physically changing in response to need, reduce demand on resources, improve function, or become multi-purpose environments.

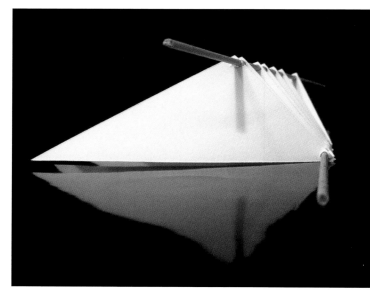

FARNAZ BAKHSHI

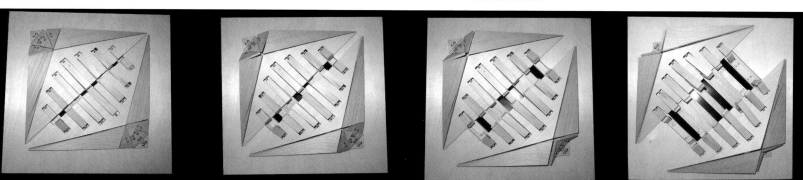

GOLNAZ BAKHSHI

PETER MCCARTHY

The use of embedded digital technologies to produce this new architecture requires an understanding of structural engineering, sensor technology and adaptable architecture. Design in the field is expanding research to many areas of multidisciplinary collaboration. This course examined the historical development of kinetic architecture and structures, explored recent research and technology applications and looked at alternative approaches to the design and conception of kinetic architecture.

PROGRAM
Threshold: A threshold is a transitional or boundary condition, a level or point at which something starts or cease to happen or come into effect.

KINETIC FUNCTION
Collapse, pivot, rotate, slide, translate, fold, expand, contract, spin, wave.

SITE
A box of one cubic foot volume.

NICHOLAS BRUSCIA

JAMES TEESE

URBAN SIMULATION

LI YIN

Benjamin Bidell
Sean Brodfuehrer
Nathan Burtch
Matthew Panasiewicz
Kevin Parris
Alex Dong Zhang

Planners and designers use computers not only to produce images, but more importantly to help systematically explore alternatives, project future patterns and trends, and communicate ideas. The Urban Simulation course was a seminar offered in spring 2005. It focused on visualization and simulation tools that were developed and applied in the environmental disciplines to facilitate better planning decisions. Under the direction of Dr. Li Yin, eight graduate students in the Department of Urban and Regional Planning and a doctoral student from the Department of Geography learned to use a variety of tools to study existing conditions, explore alternatives and their likely impacts, and uncover trends in their semester-long class projects. Tools used include ArcGIS 3D Analyst, Communityviz, Sketchup, and SiteBuilder. The level of visual enhancement and analytical capability provided by these tools and the interaction with digital models help planners and designers analyze, explore proposals and communicate their work to others. Proposals and alternatives are illustrated more efficiently with 3D simulations and real time interaction with the audience. Applying and incorporating these tools in planning practice is beneficial and integral to the effective study of complex urban systems.

LOW RISE *MID RISE* *HIGH RISE*

VISUAL ANALYSIS OF THREE REDEVELOPMENT SCENARIOS
Benjamin Bidell, Sean Brodfuehrer

Working in groups, students applied these tools in order to solve a problem that they had each identified. One group evaluated the context and potential for redevelopment relative to a site located at 235 Delaware Avenue in the city of Buffalo. They assessed three redevelopment scenarios relative to land use, construction costs, occupancy, zoning, and building context using AutoCAD, 3D Studio Max, Adobe Photoshop, ArcGIS, CommunityViz, and SiteBuilder. Another group used CommunityViz to locate trees that could potentially become hazards on Western Michigan University's campus, and to visualize this in three dimensions using ArcScene. The third group looked at three options for providing University at Buffalo students with more housing.

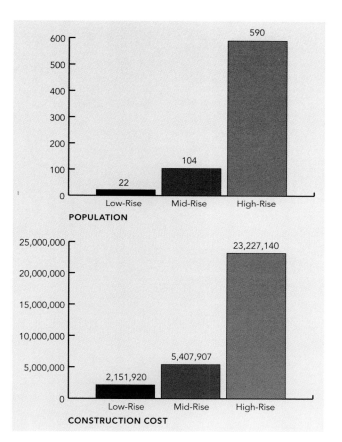

ANALYTICAL ANALYSIS OF THREE REDEVELOPMENT SCENARIOS
Benjamin Bidell, Sean Brodfuehrer

LOW RISE *MID RISE* *HIGH RISE*

HAMLIN PARK
Exposing a Community's Assets

HAMLIN PARK COMMUNITY ASSET MAP

KELLY PATTERSON

Chris Brown
Jodi Bryon
Madhulika Mukerjee
Megha Parekh
Jaclyn Patrignani

In the spring of 2005, five students in the Qualitative Methods for Planners seminar were given the assignment of developing an asset map for the Hamlin Park neighborhood. Hamlin Park is a historic African American middle class neighborhood on the eastside of Buffalo. Under the guidance of Professor Kelly Patterson, the students embarked on the task of exposing this community's assets in order to determine ways in which the community could mobilize them, build strong partnerships, and attain and maintain the stability of the neighborhood.

The goal of this project was to identify primary and secondary building blocks within Hamlin Park and to propose linkages within, and between, these building blocks. The key to the asset mapping exercise is to garner resources for community development.

The asset mapping process, developed by John P. Kretzmann and John L. Mcknight in their workbook, "Building Communities from the Inside Out," focus on the strengths and resources of a community as opposed to concentrating on its needs and problems. In their estimation, needs-based models are a detriment to communities because residents become consumers of services with no incentive to become producers. A needs-based focus also facilitates a cycle of dependence rather than empowerment.

In order to accomplish the highly complex task of asset mapping, the Hamlin Park group developed a demographic profile for the neighborhood. That included population, housing, and land use information from the U.S. Census, municipal records, and other sources. The group then conducted fieldwork in Hamlin Park to identify community-based organizations and institutions that could be linked in an associational map. The subsequent map highlighted the proposed linkages which could be formed by neighborhood groups and institutions to produce greater capacity and outcomes in community development efforts.

With the conclusion of this project, the planning document the Hamlin Park group produced serves as a resource to residents and community-based organizations, as well as a general model of asset mapping for the city of Buffalo.

HAMLIN PARK ASSET MAPPING SUMMARY

Redefining Hamlin Park

Suffering the effects of large-scale disinvestments from mid-twentieth century housing and transportation policies, Hamlin Park's streetscapes and amenities, like many found in similar central city neighborhoods throughout the country, are lackluster compared to their glittering past. However, Hamlin Park's foundation of uniformly designed streets and homes, vast tracts of green space and public space, and strong civic life remains.

Why Asset Mapping?

Today, communities are less likely to find an outside injection of dollars or expertise to begin addressing the problems in their neighborhoods. With that in mind, asset mapping offers neighborhoods a strategy to identify local resources and the talents and abilities of people already living, working, and playing there. Community asset mapping is a useful tool for neighborhoods to identify and inventory the capacities of assets in three overarching categories.

Demographic Characteristics of Hamlin Park

Despite its distinction as the first planned subdivision in the City of Buffalo and the prominence of some of its well-known residents, Hamlin Park faces a myriad of challenges as it tries to rebound from years of neglect. Decreasing vacancy and increasing levels of owner-occupied housing units are current goals of the neighborhood. Additional concerns include fostering a livable community for a substantial segment of its population who have, or are about to enter, their retirement years, as well as meeting the needs of Hamlin Park's youngest citizens, approximately 23 percent of whom are under 15 years of age.

At this time, more than 61 percent, or 772, of those residents are female. Nearly 23 percent, or 912 residents, of the population are children younger than 15, and slightly more than 19 percent of the population, or 767, are 65 years or older. African Americans are the largest ethnic group in the Hamlin Park census tract.

Assets to the Community: Organizations, Associations, Institutions and Businesses

The community and its organizations can be strengthened with a greater awareness of each others resources. The task was to help recognize the capacities and find ways to enhance existing assets. The following organizations were short listed and interviewed either in person or by telephone:

- Angel Babies
- Cornell Cooperative Extension
- Community Center of 1490 Enterprise Inc.
- Hamlin Park Community Taxpayers Association
- Hamlin Park School: Public School #74
- Lutheran Church Home
- M&T Bank
- Niagara Lutheran Home and Rehabilitation Center
- YMCA

Linkages

Two central asset connections portrayed through four asset maps, are presented as a new way for the assets of the Hamlin Park community to mutually benefit each other. The first asset map links the Hamlin Park Taxpayers Association to local churches, youth organizations, local parks and the public middle school. The second asset map links the Community Center of 1490 Enterprise, Inc. to Hamlin Park School #74, the Niagara Lutheran Home and Rehabilitation Home, the Lutheran Home, the Cornell Cooperative and M&T Bank.

Recommendations and Conclusions

The goal of this study is to recognize Hamlin Parks' assets and link them as a way of strengthening the community from within. Being a community that is already asset rich, the links are designed to specifically address the needs of the current population. Similarly, the linkages attached to the Hamlin Park Taxpayers Association are designed to address the problem of housing vacancy. This asset-based approach ensures that communities do not become dependent on external funding, thereby helping to create sustainable communities.

Event Space, Volunteer Support / Grants/Funds, Value of Volunteering

Funding, Membership / Meeting & Event Space

CONSUMING NATURE
Nature vs Culture – or – Nature and Culture?

JOYCE HWANG

Aaron Knoll
Kristin Brazinsky
James Baptiste
Steve Geltz
Dave Herbowy
Brian Goldman
Janel Bedard
Dave Taylor
Justin Hulse

The word 'nature' implies a pristine environment, one that is unaffected by civilization and society. Yet, 'culture' implies an environment which is deliberately fabricated and constructed for purposes of human use. The intersection of these two notions inevitably creates a web of seemingly conflicted logics.

Through an inquiry into the productive potential of these logics, the studio focused on strategies for redefining and intensifying 'Urban Eco-Tourism,' a system of activities which are born out of the contradictory desires to both 'consume' nature and witness its participation in the unpredictable cycle of life.

SEVEN STRATEGIES FOR URBAN-ECO TOURISM IN BUFFALO AND ERIE COUNTY

After investigating various sites of regional Urban Eco-Tourism, the studio speculated on the possibilities of enhancing existing assets (such as local natural resources) and accommodating urban desires (such as the desire to jog in the park). These speculations led to seven urban proposals, each addressing distinct conditions of ecology, consumption, and tourism.

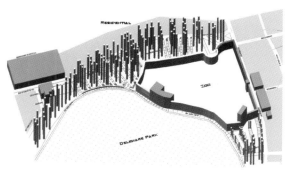

STEVE GELTZ
Zoological Gardens

As an institution which aspires to educate the public on issues pertaining to the natural world, the zoo simultaneously 'captures' the natural world in an artifice of categorizations and enclosures. Historically, zoos have attempted to shroud this blatant distinction. Rather than attempting to blend the zoo into its park-like and residential surroundings, this proposal intensifies the zoo's boundary as a thickened condition, one which intersects and distinguishes natural and artificial elements.

JUSTIN HULSE
Web of Tourism

This project recognizes the scope of Urban Eco-Tourism as one which resists automobile-based transportation while capitalizing on existing attractions promoted by tourism-driven publications. Conditions of 'walkability,' public transit opportunities, and existing nodes of attraction were systematically mapped as a web. The resulting model is an abstract tool for the siting of future development zones.

*DAVE HERBOWY
BRIAN GOLDMAN*
Industrial Heritage Trail:

Currently many of the artifacts of Buffalo's industrial heritage exist as 'ruins' along the waterfront, visited only by those who already know of their whereabouts. This project aims to increase visibility of these structures by means of a series of pedestrian, bicycle, and boating trails, linking these artifacts with existing points of attraction.

JANEL BEDARD
Low-Impact Strategies

This project advocates the use of low-impact landscaping and maintenance techniques for developing existing and potential parks in Erie County. Using a 'test site' of Emery Park, the author proposes a series of strategies, including the implementation of low-maintenance plantings initiated by an 'edible' garden of native plants, the conversion of existing 'ruined' structures into occupiable programs, and a system of converting asphalt-paved roads into pedestrian and bike trails. These techniques were then transposed to a site along the Buffalo Riverfront, one that is particular in terms of physical and social conditions.

JAMES BAPTISTE (No Image)
Seasonal Extremes

This project recommends the seasonal programming of existing parks by introducing private sponsorship of temporal activities, such as 'extreme sporting' events in the winter, urban 'camping' in the spring and summer, and county fairs in the autumn. The proposed cycle of annual activities promotes 'extreme' park usage, however only by means of temporary, incremental, and ultimately low-impact strategies.

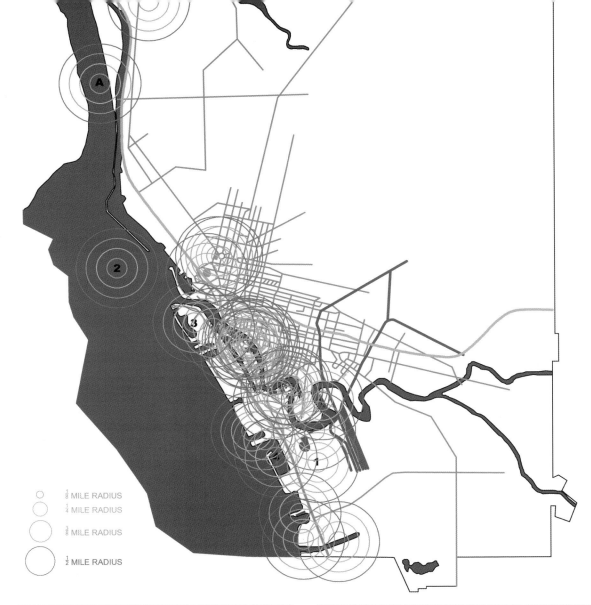

⊙ ⅛ MILE RADIUS

◯ ¼ MILE RADIUS

◯ ⅜ MILE RADIUS

◯ ½ MILE RADIUS

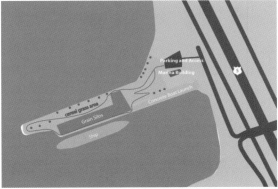

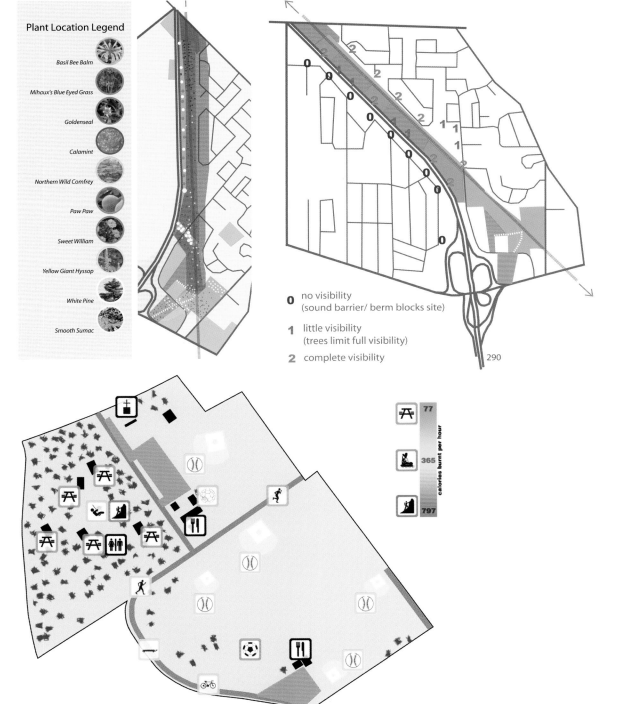

Plant Location Legend

Basil Bee Balm

Mihaux's Blue Eyed Grass

Goldenseal

Calamint

Northern Wild Comfrey

Paw Paw

Sweet William

Yellow Giant Hyssop

White Pine

Smooth Sumac

0   no visibility
    (sound barrier/ berm blocks site)

1   little visibility
    (trees limit full visibility)

2   complete visibility

290

AARON KNOLL
KRISTIN BRAZINSKY
Urban Wildlife Sanctuary

The LeClair Kindel "Wildlife Sanctuary" exemplifies the onslaught of unmaintained and relatively unvisited areas of land situated between suburban office parks, strip malls, and the thruway. This project seeks to define a strategy of introducing plant and animal species into the current 'sanctuary' and its surroundings. The project takes shape as a series of 'planting zones' in the unutiilized land along the thruway, and acts as an infrastructural connector between two commercial areas.

calories burnt per hour

77

365

797

DAVE TAYLOR
Fitness Park Regulations

This proposal capitalizes on the notion that urban parks are often utilized as sites for exercise and physical activity. Initially analyzed in terms of calorie-burning 'intensities'-- from 'calm' to 'vigorous', the Veteran's Memorial Park was re-programmed with activity-zones based on varying degrees of difficulty in traversing land topographies. The strategies used for this park suggest that a new prototype for a Fitness Park need not be based on a 'top-down' implementation of sports facilities, but rather, on tactical analyses and manipulation of existing land conditions.

THE PLAZA AT KENSINGTON HEIGHTS
An Opportunity for Large-Scale Retail Development in East Buffalo

ERNEST STERNBERG

Jill Babinski
Laila Bondi
Matt Chatfield
Constantine Giokas
Nicole McGowen
Yvette Suarez
Rich Taczkowski
Leslie Vishwanath
Austin Wheelock

SITE

The selection of a site took into account several factors related to urban retail development and the degree to which it can be successful. The site of the former Glenny Drive Apartments on Fillmore Avenue in Buffalo was chosen because it is underserved by retail and is located adjacent to the Kensington Expressway. A large, centrally located land parcel is available as are adjacent properties for possible future expansion.

SETTING

The project site is located at 1827 Fillmore Avenue near the intersection of Kensington Avenue and adjacent to the Kensington Expressway (NYS Route 33). The site has "cruciform" buildings situated on 17 acres of land. These abandoned seven-story apartment buildings are owned by the Buffalo Municipal Housing Authority. The site on the east side of Buffalo is an area divided into several territorial designations that include planning communities, councilmatic districts and legislative districts. The site is designated as the East Delavan Planning Community. It is also located in the Masten District - a predominantly African-American area. The neighborhood contains a mix of mostly 1 1/2 and 2 story housing. Residents live at income levels ranging from poor to moderate. The Masten District as a whole has pockets of well maintained homes, especially in the historic Hamlin Park neighborhood. The neighborhood contains several long standing major employers each of which brings more than 500 employees to this neighborhood.

Erie County Medical Center has a total of 2,835 employees, American Axle 1,056, Sisters of Charity Hospital 1,002, and Canisius College employs 950 people. Other businesses in the area include Sears and Roebuck Distribution Center, Rite Aid Pharmacy, Central Park Plaza, KFC, Family Dollar and several privately owned small businesses.

WHY LARGE RETAIL?

Retailers are rethinking their traditional, one-story, suburban style stores. National chains have recently opened stores in Chicago, St. Louis, Miami, Baltimore, Harlem and Brooklyn. These examples indicate that it is becoming increasingly realistic economically to build in urban areas. The movement of retailers into urban areas can benefit both the retailer and the consumer. Retail development can spur economic growth and create jobs, albeit mostly low-paying, low skill jobs. This type of development could create a range of retail shopping opportunities that do not currently exist for residents in East Buffalo. Retail plazas are perceived as unattractive because they are typically featureless and bare, and they include a vast sea of parking. However, a high quality development is feasible for this site. Innovative big box retail developments are popping up around North America and many design techniques are being used such as clustering buildings, developing shared areas, building setbacks, landscaping, energy efficient building methods, buffering, and improved sidewalks. These architectural features are both economical and elegant. Innovative design is about creatively maximizing potential. Big box retail developments need not be unsightly.

RETAIL SUPPLY

There is a shortage of good retail opportunities in the neighborhood, forcing many residents to shop outside the city and work in the surrounding suburbs. The existing retail in the Masten community is lacking in every way. Whilst the grocery category indicates that there are 56 groceries in the neighborhood, there are really only two significant groceries in the community: Tops and Save-A-Lot. The other 54 stores are small neighborhood corner stores which offer low quality and low volume. The supply is lacking and this proposed retail development would enhance the neighborhood.

RETAIL DEMAND

A market study was conducted to determine the feasibility of this project. That market research suggests that a substantial number of people can benefit from the proposed retail plaza: residents, employers and students from and visitors to local institutions, as well as commuters passing by the site. The first group which can benefit from the plaza are residents who currently travel far to pay for over-priced goods. Within a mile and a half radius of the site, these residents make up a population of over 126,000 people, living within over 52,000 households. The second group of people who would benefit from a retail plaza in East Buffalo would be those who are employed by, attend, or visit the several large institutions surrounding this site. Based on this study there is a possible consumer base of over 19,000 people. Due to the site's great visibility from the nearby highway, the third, and perhaps largest consumer base consists of the approximately 103,750 commuters who pass by the proposed retail plaza each day. Taking all of these consumer bases into consideration, suggests approximate daily capture rate between 3,000 and 10,000 shoppers.(The range is reflective of the three capture rates that were calculated: 2%, 4% and 6% per day.) This large population of shoppers will create a successful retail shopping center in East Buffalo.

INDIRECT EFFECTS

Retail development will have both positive and negative effects on local businesses in the neighborhood. It is anticipated that there will be some harm to local businesses, low-paying part-time jobs with no benefits and competition for local neighborhood stores. However it is estimated that this will be outweighed by the benefits. High prices and a lack of variety are leaving a void in the

neighborhood. Family Dollar and Dollar General stores that are located in the neighborhood are national chains, and they are less likely to be affected by this proposed development. This study concludes that the Central Park Plaza would not be in direct competition with the proposed new plaza and will have minimal effect on businesses located there since the trend at Central Park Plaza is towards attracting office and service tenants, not retail. Large scale retail has the potential to create jobs and may act as a catalyst by supporting small stores. There will be increased investment and traffic in the area, which will increase neighborhood activity and pride in the community. Retail development in Buffalo will inevitably stem the flow of urban dollars to suburban locations. Ideally, a retail plaza would augment other businesses and not compete. This outcome cannot be guaranteed. Our best judgment is that some may be harmed, but that others will be helped.

HIGHWAY ACCESS

The site for the Plaza at Kensington Heights is in an ideal location in terms of highway and street transportation accessibility. Good connections exist near a limited access highway, and there are excellent links to major arterial roads and local streets. Currently, there are several ways to enter and exit the site. However, the site lacks an immediate interchange with the Kensington Expressway (NYS Route 33) at Fillmore Avenue, making access indirect. Therefore, alternatives have been proposed. One alternative seeks to improve highway access by simplifying the route between the site and existing interchanges. To do this, a two way road would need to be constructed along the northern perimeter of the site, beginning at Fillmore Avenue. This road would connect with the access road passing through the northern portion of the Erie County Medical Center campus. This road

HIGHWAY TRAFFIC VOLUMES

Road	Segment	Daily Traffic Count (Yr)
Fillmore Avenue	Delavan Ave. to Kensington Ave.	11,000 (2003)
Kensington Avenue	Main St. to Fillmore Ave.	6,500 (2003)
	Fillmore Ave. to Grider St.	8,400 (2002)
East Delavan Avenue	Humboldt Pkwy. to Fillmore Ave.	9,400 (2003)
	Fillmore Ave. to Grider St.	8,000 (2003)
Main Street (NYS Route 5)	Delavan Ave. to Route 198	20,000 (2001)
	Route 198 to Jewett Pkwy.	14,500 (2002)
East Ferry Street	Humboldt Pkwy. to Fillmore Ave.	10,000 (2003)
	Fillmore Ave. to Grider St.	9,100 (2004)

ARTERIAL TRAFFIC VOLUMES

intersects Grider Street where, one block north, a highway interchange is located. Another way to create direct access to the site is by constructing new exit and entrance ramps on Fillmore Avenue. With the construction of these new ramps, roads would also have to be constructed to create a safe environment for vehicular traffic. Regardless of the alternative improvements and changes will have to be made to have direct access to the site. Even without direct site access, it should be noted that the area is currently commercially viable because entrances and exits already exist. Nevertheless, immediate highway access is preferable.

COMMUNITY ACCESS

Personal vehicles will be the predominant means of transportation to and from the plaza, but transit and pedestrian access are also important. The Niagara Frontier Transit Authority has two Metro Rail stations within 1/2 mile of the site. Existing bus services are

also a viable option for gaining access to The Plaza at Kensington Heights. The closest current stop is on Route 23, at the intersection of North Fillmore Avenue and Glenny Drive. Alternate routes are near the proposed plaza, with stops at the Erie County Medical Center and Seneca Vocational High School. Upon completion of the development, it is expected that the bus service will be rerouted. In terms of bicycle and pedestrian access, there is a network of routes surrounding the development site, and though they need improvement, there are existing sidewalks.

FITTING INTO EXISTING PLANS

The proposed retail plaza complements and builds upon other plans for the region. The proposals for this site are in tune with Buffalo's Comprehensive Plan, the East Delavan Good Neighbors Planning Alliance Neighborhood Plan, the Masten District Neighborhood Plan, the Fillmore Business District Commercial Project, the Scajaquada Corridor Study and Olmsted Plans and the needs and wants of the community.

PARCELS

The entire project area is made up of seven groupings of parcels, referred to as blocks A-F, whose current use and/or proximity to the primary site makes them reasonable considerations for redevelopment. The project area is bounded on the west by the active CSX railroad line and on the east by Erie County Medical

SITE PEDESTRIAN ACCESS

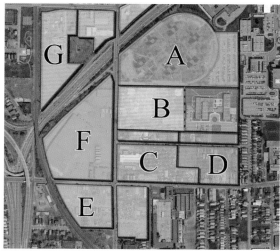

BLOCK DIAGRAM

SCHEMATIC PROPOSAL 1

SCHEMATIC PROPOSAL 2

Center (ECMC) and Chelsea Place. Kensington Avenue acts as the northern boundary of the project area, with the exception of a strip along the east side of the rail line extending north to Leroy Avenue. The southern boundary is East Delavan Avenue, except for block E, which spans Fillmore Avenue south of East Delavan Avenue towards Boardman Avenue (see block diagram). The seven blocks are comprised of 124 parcels on 99.73 acres of land:

> 7 industrial parcels
> 33 commercial parcels
> 38 residential parcels
> 42 vacant parcels
> 4 public/institutional land parcels

The primary parcel for The Plaza at Kensington Heights is the vacant public housing project on Fillmore Avenue, between Delavan and Kensington Avenues. This readily available publicly owned site offers over 17 contiguous acres with proximity to Route 33. The primary site is also adjacent to an additional thirteen acres of public lands. In addition, the surrounding neighborhood is a mixture of moderate to under-utilized institutional, industrial, commercial, residential and vacant properties, bringing the total overall project area to approximately one hundred acres.

CONCEPTUAL DESIGN GUIDES

The project design presents alternative concepts through the progression of three different development phases, looking to meet the immediate and future retail needs of the East Buffalo community. These concepts serve as a design guide for an urban retail development in East Buffalo community. Design of both the site and the buildings should recognize three goals:

- Address the street frontage with transparent building façades.
- Create centralized programmable community space.
- Consider pedestrian and transit access both internal and external to the site.

The proposals embody these recommendations within a development scheme focused on new forms for urban shopping.

LESLIE STREET SPIT BOAT HOUSE

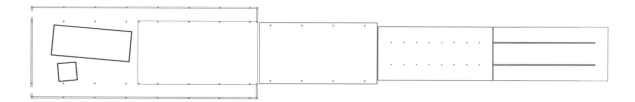

TORBEN BERNS

William Helm
Rachel Stecker

The six-week studio was intended to link a particular attitude to site with an appropriate program. The site for the project was the Leslie Street Spit, a 5 km spit of landfill originally constructed to enlarge Toronto's harbor, but which, following an economic downturn in shipping, was designated as a conservation park and wetland experiment. The wetlands themselves are created out of carefully controlled "clean fill" from construction waste, producing one of the most original and successful conservation sites on Lake Ontario. The program as given was the relocation of the Toronto Rowing Club boathouse.

The project was introduced first as Container A (with Contents A) moving in both plan and section into Container B where the contents of A are released.

Students were asked to create a narrative regarding possible choreographies and transformations as recorded by a specific index. Both the contents of "A" and the index were to be "derivatives" of the site. The size of Container B was 1' X 1' X 1'.

Following the initial investigation, the project was posed again as a boathouse for the rowing club with the programmatic requirements of storing 30 sculls, change rooms for 20 people, docking facilities and administration. The attitude to the site became the means of reconciling the necessities of the boathouse with the demands of the site. The relation between the two was a corollary to the principles of sustainability introduced earlier in the semester.

RACHEL STECKER, BOATHOUSE PLAN (TOP), ANIMATED BOATHOUSE MODEL (ABOVE)

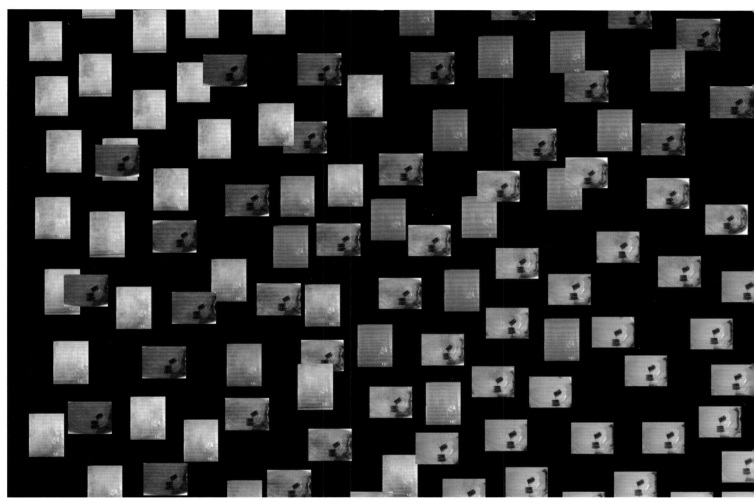

RACHEL STECKER, DECIPHER (ABOVE)

Contents A: Tea leaves
Container A: Tea Bag
Container B: Water

The tea transforms the water differently each time The infusion/transformation rate of the water to tea is based on the ratio of the quantity of tea to the total quantity of water. Both the tea leaves and the water end up transforming each other through the process. The steeping of the tea is captured on video.
Each frame of the video is then captured and used to graphically describe the transformation process.

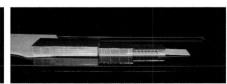

RACHEL STECKER

This project uses the idea of movement and transformation to create a building that responds to both programmatic and seasonal changes. As a rowing club, most of the building is used for boat storage and docking space. Both of these are necessary primarily in spring and summer months. The largest segment of the building functions as a shell that can house the other segments of the building during winter months. Starting with the dock, the segments slide out and extend to the full, functional length exposing the boat and oar storage. The building is purposely translucent to act as a lighthouse on the coast of the Leslie Street Spit. The exposure of program and lightness allows the building not just to be readable in the landscape but also to be a way of marking the opening and closing of seasons.

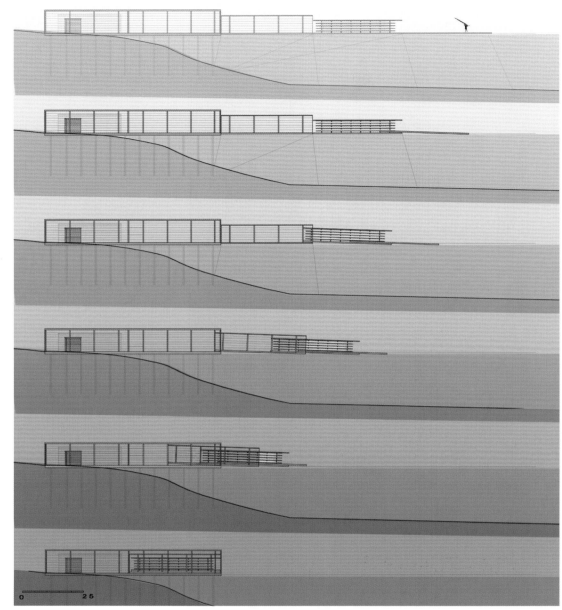

0   25

BOATHOUSE ELEVATION (ABOVE)

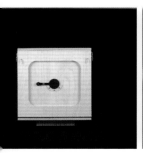   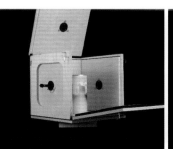 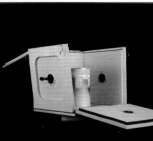

WILLIAM HELM

In 1791 Jeremy Bentham proposed the theory of the Panopticon as a solution for a detention center with maximum surveillance capabilities. In the same decade in England, Thomas Wedgewood and Humphry Davy used a camera obscura in their attempts to fix an image onto paper, leather and glass coated with a silver nitrate solution.

These two phenomena are combined in the Pinhole Panopticon. It is conceptualized as an installation that records the space in which it is installed and opens to display the process in which the recording process took place. At its core, is a cylindrical film plane on which the projected image circles from the four sides blend together at their extremities. The result is a complex record of the surrounding space. The resultant image is panoramic in typology, but not definition. Each projected image is inverted in both axes so that the overlapping edges do not coincide with each other. The result is an agglomeration of intersecting space from opposing sides of the room.

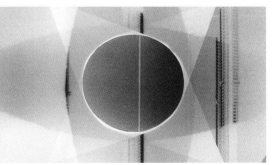

FINAL IMAGE (TOP), PINHOLE PANOPTICON (ABOVE), UNFOLD SEQUENCE (BELOW)

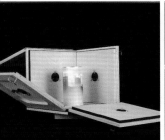

WILLIAM HELM

The boathouse investigates the concept of the motion blur. The blur can be both the blur of the background with a subject in focus, or the blurring of the subject within a static environment. The program was researched through the observation of the UB Crew team from the coaching craft. From this a 3:00 minute film short was developed of moving imagery from the site and the program investigations. Footage of the program and the site are jump cut together using an inversely proportionate time sequence. A multi-layered audio soundtrack is composed of breaking waves from the site and an eight-man scull moving across the water.

The proposal explores how the structure of the construct can establish rhythms similar to that of the scull moving across the water's surface. The constants are longitudinal bearing walls. The roof starts as a flat plane but forms a central valley that steadily drops along the longitudinal axis. In doing so, the eaves sweep gently upward producing a compound curve in the roof plates. The proposal is a two building facility. First - a non climate controlled boathouse and workshop - has been sheared away from the main building that remains embedded in the shoreline. The boathouse housing thirty sculls is pulled into the water, easing the launching of sculls.

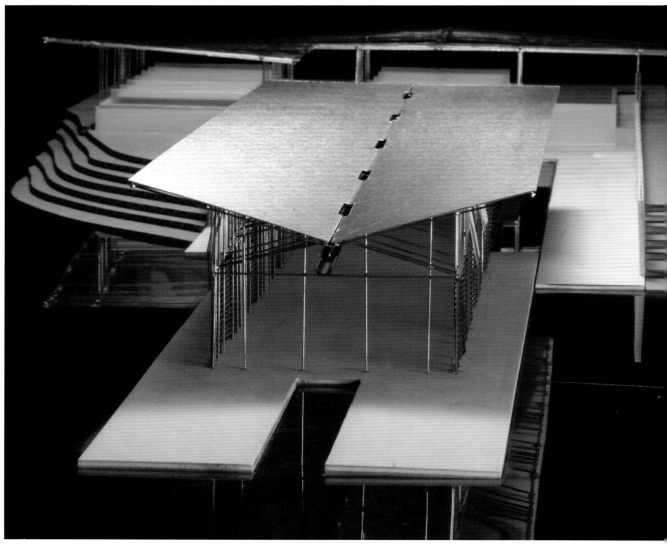

PROGRAM + SITE ANALYSIS (TOP), BOATHOUSE IN THE FOREGROUND IS PULLED AWAY FROM OTHER PROGRAM (ABOVE)

SCULLS ARE LAUNCHED FROM THE TWO SIDES OF THE BOATHOUSE (ABOVE)

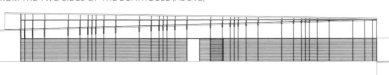

ELEVATION

DESIGN STUDIO 503 . FALL 2004

STEVEN HOLL WITH GRADUATE STUDENTS AT THE ELLICOTT SQUARE BUILDING IN BUFFALO AND WITH CHRIS AND SALLY MARTELL (BELOW LEFT)

2005 MARTELL DISTINGUISHED VISITING CRITIC
Steven Holl Architects

"I am as interested in books as buildings. Making a book is like making a building. It takes a lot of effort and is agonizing, but somehow also very fulfilling because you have to make things coalesce."

Steven Holl, Martell Lecture, April 2005

STEVEN HOLL
MARTIN COX

In 2004 Christopher Martell and his wife Sally generously agreed to support a new Martell Distinguished Visiting Critic Program – a program directed at bringing architects of international significance to the School of Architecture and Planning at the University at Buffalo each year to teach in the graduate program, give a school-wide public lecture and assist in preparing a publication that documents that lecture for a wider audience.

The program connects the School to architectural practices of global significance and brings the design insights and professional experiences of those practices into our studios, seminar rooms and lecture halls. Aimed to inspire the entire community of students, yet enable individuals to benefit from the intimacy of working with gifted visitors, the program is designed to bring outstanding architects to the University at Buffalo.

Steven Holl Architects was appointed as the Martell Distinguished Visiting Critic in the 2004-2005 academic year. During the Spring 2005 semester, Steven Holl and his associate Martin Cox worked with students in a comprehensive graduate design studio. The inaugural Martell Lecture was given in Buffalo in April, 2005 by Steven Holl and published as a Buffalo Book in the Fall 2005 semester.

MARTIN COX, DESIGN REVIEW

WILLIAM HELM, TRANSPORTER II, NOAA-VLA, SOCORRO, NM

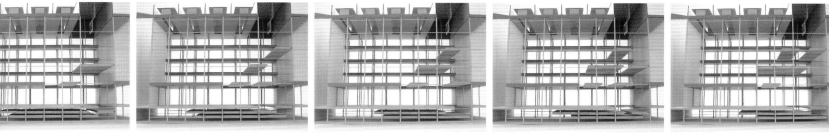

WILLIAM HELM; SECTIONAL ANIMATION

ARTIFACT
Martell Distinguished Visiting Critic Studio

"Architectural thought is the working through of phenomena initiated by idea...Whether reflecting on the unity of concept and sensation or the intertwining of idea and phenomena, the hope is to unite intellect and feeling, precision with soul."

Steven Holl, Anchoring, 1991

STEVEN HOLL
MARTIN COX
STEVEN HOLL ARCHITECTS
ANNETTE LECUYER
BRAD WALES

Simon Braun-Kolbe
Joe Carline
William Helm
Rachel Stecker

MARTIN COX, DESIGN REVIEW

In a letter to a group of South African modern architects noted in the preface to the first volume of *Oeuvre Complete (1910-1929)*, Le Corbusier wrote of the critical importance of reaching beyond the self-referential conventions of normal professional practice in search of fresh inspiration for a new architecture. In particular, he noted, "The architect must become the most sensitive and best informed of art lovers", in order not to run the risk of " an intelligence as hermetically sealed by professional specialism as that of grocers."

I was reminded of Le Corbusier's letter while reflecting on the Spring semester of 2005, when I had the privilege of participating in the graduate studios as part of the Martell Distinguished Visiting Critic Program. The project, a Museum of Contemporary Art, offered a rich and complex challenge to the students: a large public building with multiple layers of organizational relationships; two very different corner sites with a variety of urban scalar conditions; and spatial typologies such as the gallery requiring specific interior qualities. Most importantly, the project seemed to demand that each student take a position on the overarching cultural questions of the relationships between art and architecture, the museum and the city.

This understanding of architecture as being situated in the broader culture, interdependent with and drawing on the practices and discoveries of other disciplines, is a central aspiration of the approach of Steven Holl Architects, as illustrated by two particular buildings discussed during the semester. For Kiasma, the Museum of Contemporary Art of Finland, the designated site was an urban sliver of leftover space at a pinch point where the city and the surrounding civic monuments of the National Parliament, the Central Post Office and Eliel Saarinen's Railway Station were cut off from the landscape of Töölö Bay by obsolete railyards. The design began with the concept of "chiasma," or intertwining, a term that links the philosophy of phenomenology with the biological aspects of vision and perception. In the building, a spatial knot weaves the gallery sequence into the city. As the body moves through the space

MARTELL STUDIO . SPRING 2005

WILLIAM HELM

The museum is designed as a platform of maximum flexibility in configuration. Embedded in the concept is the desire for simultaneous interactive storage and display that can be reconfigured for each exhibition. The design has two components: Infrastructure, and Machine. The museum becomes the infrastructure upon which the machines navigate the site -- similar to the NOAA-VLA transporter used in Soccoro, New Mexico. The main gallery measures 72' wide by 142' long, with a volume of 750,000 cubic feet. The intent is to commission artists to create work designed specifically for this space. A north/south light well cuts a section cleanly through the entire museum. The industrial landscape of roof monitors distributes light throughout the gallery volume. The north and south facades are pulled away from the floor plates to become freestanding hybrid systems supported by 90 foot vertical trusses. On the north side, the outer layer is an open jointed etched glass rainscreen with an interior layer of butt jointed glazing to act as a thermal barrier. On the south facing system, a layer of operable sunshade louvers is placed on the exterior of the glazed barrier to minimize heat gain.

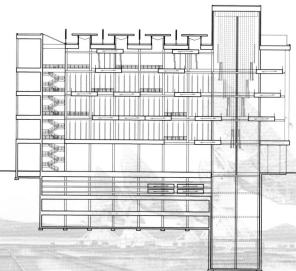

of the museum, the experience of art becomes enmeshed with the experience of the building, the urban situation and the new opening of the city to the landscape. Similarly, a current project for the design of the new School of Art and Art History at the University of Iowa began with the aspiration of a building for art practice and education imbued with new understandings of space proposed by art. The project is conceived as being formed of planar space, open at the edges to the outside and with indeterminate boundaries. Early model explorations - studies of abstract spatial conditions free of structure or program - were informed by understandings of space as implied by planar assemblies proposed by Pablo Picasso, Naum Gabo and others.

Over the course of the semester an impressive range of approaches emerged in the studio, informed by the seemingly infinite variables of the given scenario. Many students' schemes were primarily driven by investigations of the urban issues posed by the project and the question of the public building in the contemporary city, a discourse that was intensified by the seemingly innocuous inclusion of a housing component in the program. This proved pivotal as the studio's work evolved and students realized the frictions inherent in this ingredient, which forced a confrontation between seemingly incompatible programmatic imperatives. For some this fueled a reinvention of the museum typology; one student imagined resident, almost captive, artists haunting the galleries at night after paying visitors had left while others resolved the tensions through urban design strategies.

A number of students produced provocative work that reached beyond elegant fulfillment of the given parameters and towards a critical re-examination of the cultural role and conventions of the contemporary museum, proposing buildings that were the result of approaches to collecting and exhibiting that are radically different to conventional practice. While supermuseums such as the MoMA may present less than 10% of their collections at any one time, and these in curated exhibitions, these projects sought

MUSEUM LEVELS

Meeting Rooms
Art Viewing
Residences
Library

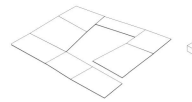 

Offices
Gallery
Storage
Residences

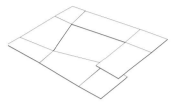  

Offices
Gallery
Storage

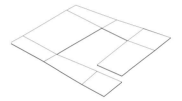 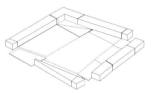 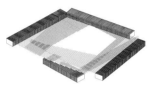

Entry
Classrooms
Lecture Hall
Gift Shop
Sculpture Gallery
Gallery
Storage

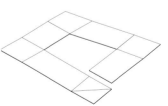 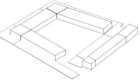  

GALLERY SEQUENCE   *ART STORAGE & DISPLAY*

RACHEL STECKER

This project investigates the public-private relationship in the museum by creating a new way for art and people to circulate in the same spaces. The corner location of the site allows for the wrapping of different types of circulation that begin outside the building with the automobile and pedestrian and continue to the core of the building where the gallery visitor views the art.

The form of the building is an abstraction of the site. Each layer is divided based on programmatic requirements. The floors gradually slope, creating a continuous ramp starting at the sidewalk. The museum becomes an extension of the urban surroundings.

The program is organized in vertical layers that wrap an interior core of light. The program is divided into support services (outermost ring), storage, and gallery (inner ring). The concentric nature of these layers creates functional proximity in the gallery, allowing a more intimate understanding of the museum. Public and private spaces are linked by the cross movement of the art in and out of its storage space.

JOE CARLINE

Traditionally, the ground is understood as the frame onto which architecture is erected. In this investigation, the figure-ground relationship is changed. The ground is mastered. The earth is no longer understood as the object on which to build; it is now the subject and a tectonic element.

The project is an intervention into the network of public spaces of Allentown. By reclaiming the ground plane for socialization, a connection between Allentown, its public and the museum/study center is established. Through the manipulation of the surface plane, the ground is optimized to include a summer reflecting pool, winter ice skating rink, outdoor cinema screen, public seating area and green space. Exploration of the plasticity of the ground challenges the preconception that it is inherently stable or a constant datum.

The key to understanding the museum's program is revealed on the surface through translucent glass volumes. Like a stone in a Zen garden, the literal nature of the glass volume is abstracted; it is an object of contemplation. Each glass volume, which provides diffuse daylight to the galleries below, is an extrusion of a structural wall. From within, the folded surface appears to float.

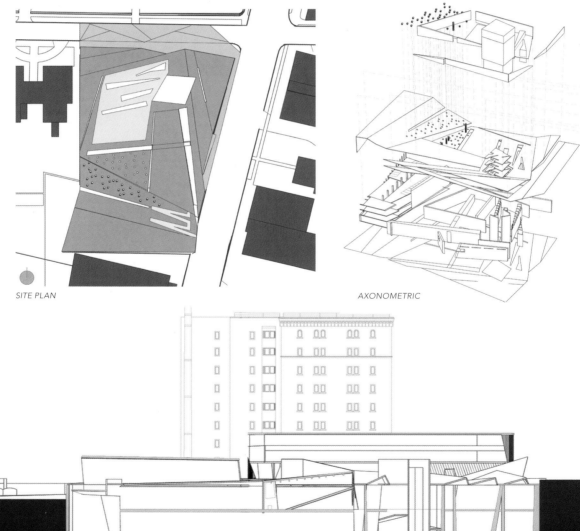

SITE PLAN

AXONOMETRIC

to dissolve the boundaries between "collection" and "exhibition", in other words between public and private, curated and unedited. Other students drew directly on their study of contemporary art, encouraged by the requirement of studying the work of a given artist, and their own artistic practices to propose innovative spatial models for the museum that similarly questioned current conventions.

Le Corbusier's design process, which he famously described as a *récherche patiente*, was an integration of artistic, architectural and intellectual disciplines expressly intended as a method for cross-fertilization of ideas and the prevention of an overly narrow focus on the normal terms of reference of the profession. The practice of painting, and his associations with artists such as Ozenfant and Leger were key to his innovations. His exhortations to the aspiring South Africans seem even more urgent today as the traditional boundaries of the creative professions are increasingly eroded: Bruce Mau designs an urban presence for a new football stadium in New York, while artists Jorge Pardo and Andrea Zittel design and build houses that exist in between "art" and "architecture." Architecture, its practice and products, have become a focus of investigation and aesthetic dissection for many artists. Working in this cultural context, with the ground shifting under our feet, it is through an engagement and realignment of architecture with other cultural disciplines that architecture will maintain a critical role and innovations will emerge.

The opportunity to step outside our practice in New York City - for regular infusions of intellectual stimulation and inspiration in Buffalo led to the realization that the unspoken secret of the *récherche patiente* in the studio is that students are in fact teaching the critics.

Martin Cox, Steven Holl Architects

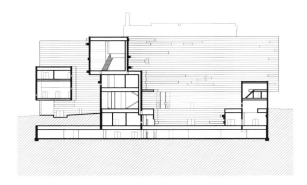

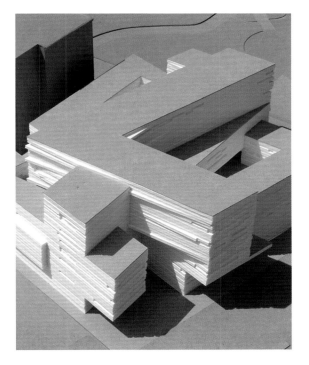

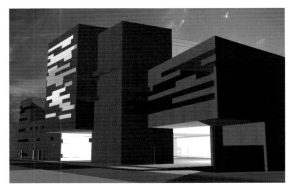

SIMON BRAUN-KOLBE

The streets bounding the site are linked to the natural and cultural topography of Buffalo. North Street, once the city's northern edge, is located on the Onondaga Limestone Escarpment, which creates a natural threshold to the city.

The form of the plan is derived from the angle of the bounding streets, and the geography of the site is extruded to become a building comprised of strata. The stratified building becomes a landmark or boundary stone. A range of public spaces is 'carved' into the layers. The galleries are situated at the top of this constructed escarpment so as to fix the gaze of visitors on adjacent historic buildings, thus connecting the new museum specifically to the urban landscape.

Site cast concrete strata 2.5 feet in thickness are used to build loadbearing walls. The concrete, exposed inside and out, is an insulated cavity wall. The strata are emphasized by an iron additive in the concrete mix. As the building weathers, the metal will oxidize to color the concrete in hues that will continue to evolve during the life of the building. Weathering inside will not occur as quickly as on the outside. The sedimentary layers can be split into sub-strata of 6 inches in order to create stairs or layered windows of cast glass.

SELF ORGANIZING SYSTEMS
Reorganizing Nervi's GWB Bus Terminal

OMAR KHAN
ALISA ANDRASEK

Matthew Zinski
Dirk Pfeifer
Cesar Cedano
Daniel Gallagher
Seth Amman

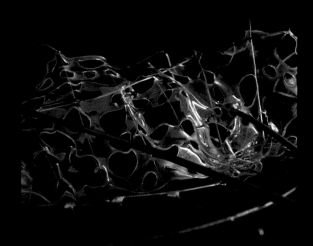

Self Organization is an emerging characteristic of dynamic systems. Whether these are natural or man-made they exhibit the ability to accommodate change, maintain equilibrium and evolve new structures. Students began by diagramming the behavior of such natural/cultural systems to understand and analyze their self-organizing principles. Concurrently, using Maya modeling software they created a series of spatial studies that used 2D and 3D arrays to simulate changes across a "field". These studies became the basis for generating spatial and programmatic organizations that use the initial natural/cultural studies as analogies as well as instruments.

Pier Luigi Nervi's George Washington Bridge Bus Terminal is a unique structure that attempts to negotiate a variety of dynamic conditions presented by its site. Large urban arteries like the George Washington Bridge, the Cross Bronx Expressway and Broadway are integrated into the building's design, whose success primarily lies in the way it handles vehicular traffic. Arguably less success can be seen in its negotiation of pedestrian movement and integration into its residential neighborhood. The terminal became a means to explore reorganization of an existing transit system with the addition of a hotel that provides accommodation on an hourly, daily and weekly basis. The students were given the option of renovating the terminal or proposing an alternative on the same site footprint.

DIRK PFEIFER

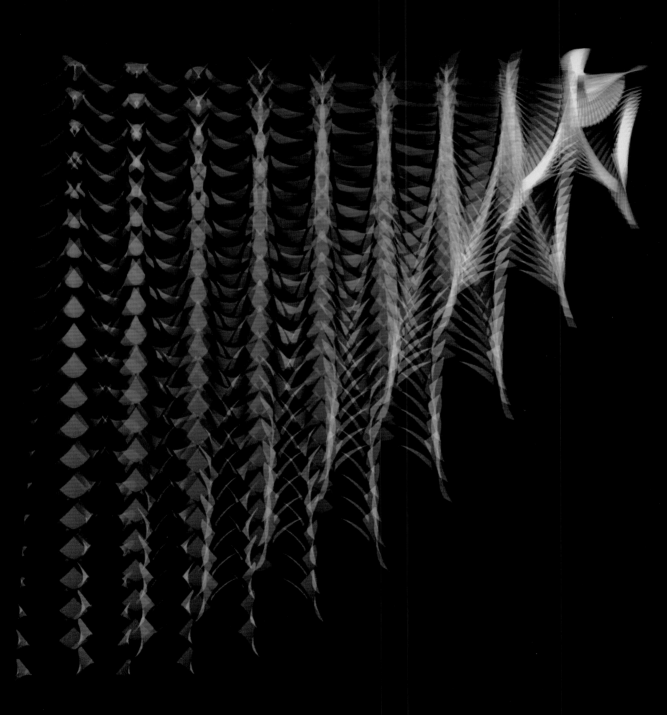

DIRK PFEIFER

Based on earlier investigations on phase shifting matter (solid to liquid to gas) I experimented with spatial distortions resulting from acceleration and deceleration. This concept was applied to building material transitions from heavy concrete to light carbon fiber structures, which emphasized the changing porosity of the façade, as well as the time based program of transitional spaces from long term hotel facilities to short break commuter lounges. An important design decision was to play with the perception of material change and also to use "immaterial" change from dark to bright spaces, variation in air pressures, and the pace and quantity of people moving through space to create interactive densities.

GRADUATE DESIGN STUDIO . FALL 2004

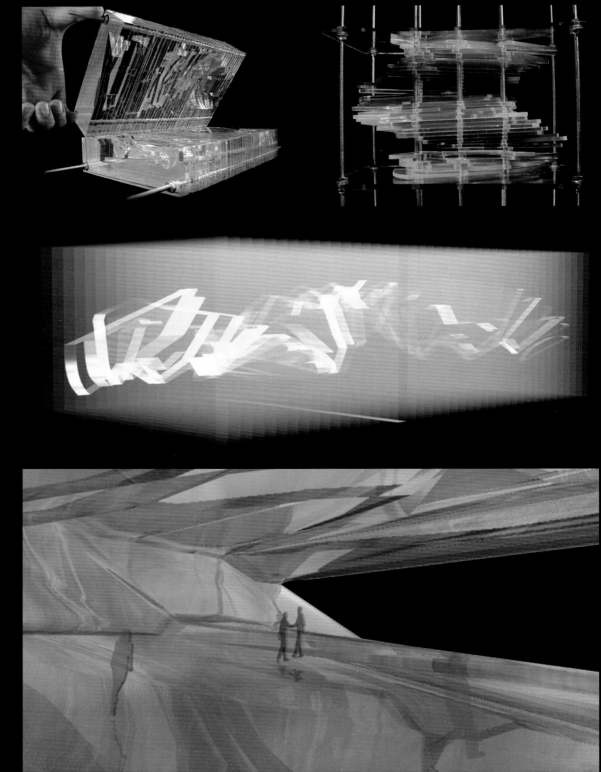

CESAR CEDANO

Through an analysis of user interaction with BitTorrent, a file sharing system, a series of studies was produced that demonstrated the network's similarities to self-replicating cell systems. These were deployed in the site using BitTorrent's rules and regulations to create a spatial construct. By sectioning the spatial program a series of situations was generated that helped to determine the organization of use and program. The sectioning also provided ease of handling the program's complexity by creating associations between parts. These became generators of form and framework for the hotel and bus terminal.

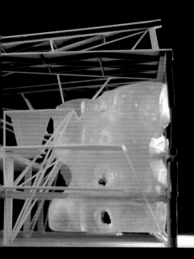

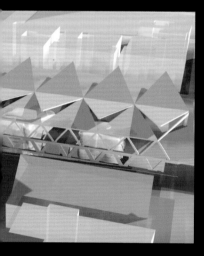

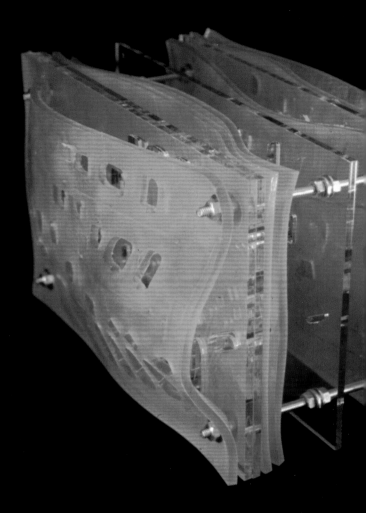

also termed agents) come together under a rule set
hitectural implications of such a system are made
ate programs, bus station and hotel within one
Bridge Bus Terminal. The agents of the Nervi Bus
nd react with the hotel agents (form, structure, and
at responds to each element's shifting intelligence
mally interweaving and structurally acrobatic and
al violence. The violent organizational interaction
ry negotiations.

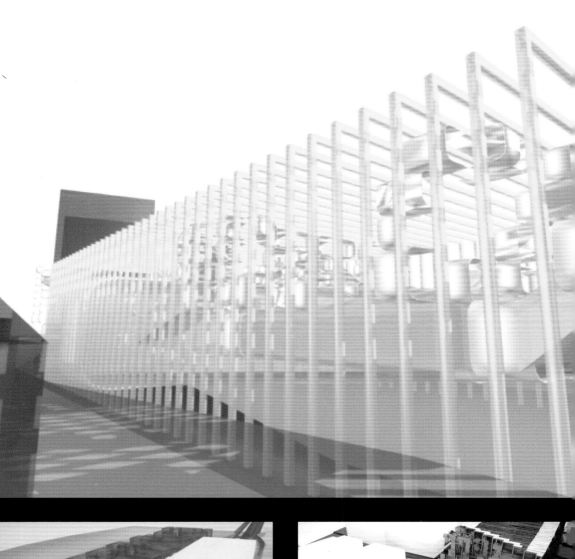

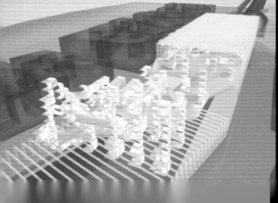

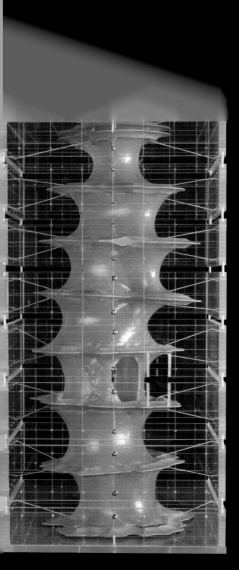

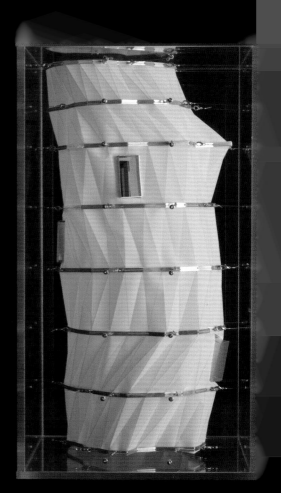

BRUCE GIBSON

MIN LI / QI WANG

In Buffalo, as in many post-industrial cities, the issue of reclaiming existing urban fabric is arguably more pressing than that of new construction. The prevailing conceptual framework for reinhabiting existing structures – "adaptive reuse" is its common name – explicitly privileges a smooth alignment between reuse and structure, casting terms such as rupture, friction, misfit as naturally negative values when mating a new programmatic identity to an existing body. Smooth alignment is not just a code

for economic viability – friction being associated with inefficiency – but also supports a image of might be termed "reversed continuity," whereb future appropriation of the city progressively m towards an (imagined) past, akin to the trajecto boomerang.

This studio embraced both adaptive reuse as a mode of urban revalidation, and friction and mi potentially positive architectural conditions. St

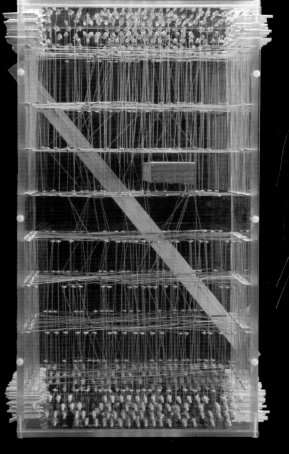

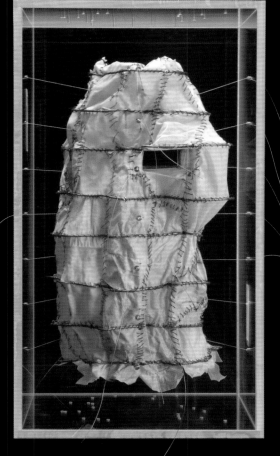

ERIN COX / GARRETT WYCKOFF

JOE CARLINE / WILLIAM HELM

BOX | LADY

explored these issues in two exercises: the first ("Box/Lady") involved the conflation of two disparate formal conditions – an acrylic box and a fragment of the Statute of Liberty; the second ("Hand/Shoe") involved the conflation of one of Buffalo's most renowned architectural figures – Sullivan's Guaranty Building – with a program for a new school of architecture, a program that in size and type intentionally denied a hand/glove fit with the former office building.

Working in teams of two, students were asked to support eight planimetric sections of the Statue of Liberty In a vertical box of 3/8" thick acrylic measuring 20" x 11" x 11". They then interpolated and clad the region between the sections with a sheet material of their choice. The acrylic box additionally was to have two pairs of openings to permit two 1" x 2" prismatic voids to pass uninterrupted through the entire piece.

"The Prudential Building was originally designed as an office building. The Task Force has assumed throughout this study that offices represent the best continued use for the building...."

HAND | SHOE

In 1977, in response to the pending demolition of Louis Sullivan's 1895 Prudential (originally Guaranty) Building, a Task Force was formed to devise a plan for the reuse and restoration of the building. Among other findings, the Task Force determined that the size and configuration of the original floor plates were serious obstacles to contemporary office use. To rectify this condition, the Task Force recommended infilling the building's light court. In the early 1980s this measure was realized.

Neither the proposed reuse as contemporary office space, nor the proposed architectural modifications, were conceptualized as positive change. Instead, both recommendations were framed in terms of preservation in which, ironically, change was valued as a means of maximizing authenticity. Office use was framed as an original use, and modifying the floor plates was framed as enabling the return to an original use.

Despite this calculus, both the new use of the Prudential Building as contemporary office space and the new configuration of the building's floor plates can fairly be termed "radical." The use was sufficiently at odds with the original program of the building so as to necessitate an architectural intervention which effected nothing less than a fundamental transformation of the building's organizational logic. This project was premised on the notion that such radicalism can be fruitfully understood, embraced, and expressed, as mark of urban and architectural vitality. Following the example, if not the spirit, of the Task Force, the Prudential Building (1977 condition) was the site for exploring - and celebrating - the architectural potential of mismatched adaptive reuse. The students were asked to house a program for an architecture school of approximately 84,000 net square feet in the Prudential Building which has a net area of approximately 78,000 square feet (1977 condition).

MIN LI

To house a program for an architectural school into the Prudential Building, this project aims not only to bring life back to the old building and its environment, but also to create a place expressing openness to the public. In order to answer such wish, this project distributes studio space through one continuous spiral ramp, eliminating the concept of layers, inserted into rigid existing floor spaces. In a cityscape of vertical and straight lines, the freshness of spiral and circles break out of cellular subdivisions of existing spaces and add a new dimension to the Prudential Building. New volumes are shifted corresponding to its environment, also allowing light and air to come into studio spaces. Behaviors and activities in this continuous spiral space are revealed to the public through transparent and translucent building skins, which adds an attractive scene to the city.

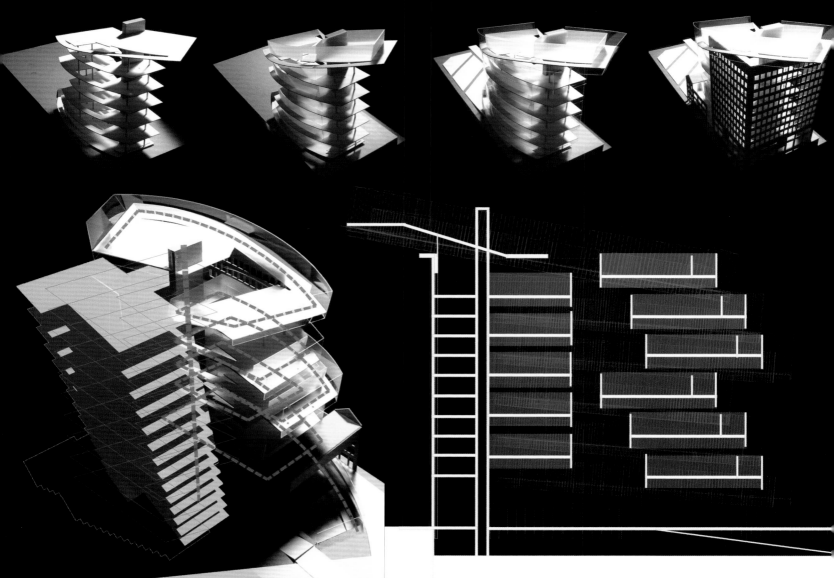

MICHAEL NOWAK

The design solution for a new school of architecture to be located in the Guaranty Building was grounded in a study of the hierarchical nature of the terra-cotta tile work on the original facade and applied a hierarchical system of structure that inversed the nature of skin and structure. The solution consisted of a primary, secondary, and tertiary system of structural elements, which unlike the original rational and orthogonal structure of columns and beams, reacted to local forces to determine the final building form. The solution to the program requirements placed the graduate studios outside the Guaranty Building proper. All structure was strictly outside the surface of the studio facade/skin. The tertiary and secondary structural cables stabilized the floor & ceiling planes of the studios relative to each other. The Primary structure of steel tubes reacted against these tensile force elements and the shape was determined by the locations of the studios.

INTERIOR DENSITY

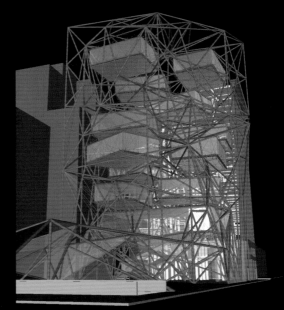

PEARL STREET RENDERING

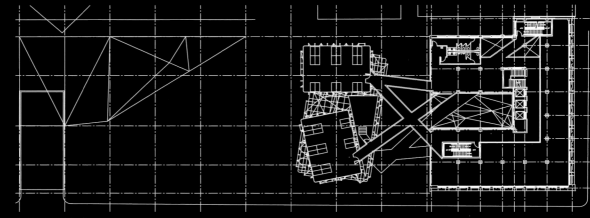

FIFTH FLOOR PLAN

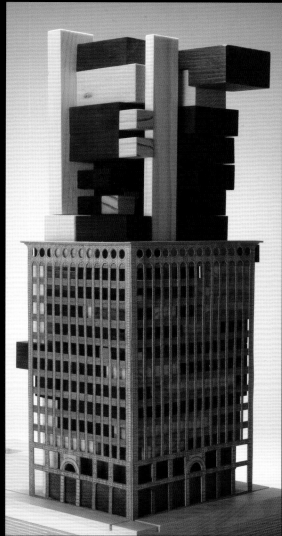

1/16" MASSING/CLADDING STUDY MODEL

PHOTOGRAM

PEARL STREET RENDERING

1/32" SITE MODEL

WILLIAM HELM

Parallax occurs with the insertion of a program that does not align in plan and section with the spatiality of a room intended as an office. This new proposal allows the program to engage the original terra cotta facades only when its occupancy aligns with Sullivan's original intentions. Where it does not align, Sullivan's module is used to carve appropriate spaces for the remaining programmatic elements. This operation pushes an already oversized program out of the existing envelope. A new glazed thermal undergarment is exposed that must be veiled with the detailing of a new outer garment. The new thermal barrier and program engage the new cladding system in a similar way that the terra cotta facade is engaged. Steel perforation patterns were replicated on transparent materials and rotated in tandem between an enlarger and photosensitive paper to replicate the daylight effects throughout the year. The resulting images give clues to the effects within the new spaces. The perception the construct is fluid yet phantasmic as a person's aspect to the Guaranty changes.

FINAL THESIS REVIEW

MEASURING THE TIDAL EFFECT OF SPACE

Christopher Romano

MEHRDAD HADIGHI
THESIS CHAIR

JEAN LA MARCHE
THESIS COMMITTEE

This thesis investigates a critical tectonic event, the interaction of architecture and site. The task of the architect in this proposal, is to create an architecture of context by revealing the nature of the site through calibrated modifications of its material conditions, leading to a productive utilization of the landscape. The role of the architect, in this proposal, is to be an astute observer and a precise analyst of the landscape.

The relationship between architecture and context has been a long-standing philosophical question. This thesis is a challenge to the architect concerning the interaction of building and landscape. The act of construction is destined to produce a new landscape and thus architects have the responsibility to draw out the particular characteristics of a given landscape. The purpose of this thesis is to provoke the static relationship of site and building in favor of a more dynamic one that is, finally, the production of architecture.

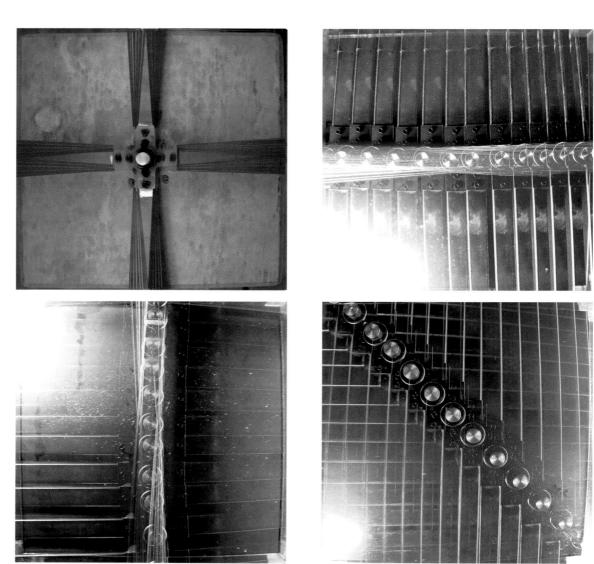

RECORD OF MOVEMENT, 4 PIERS

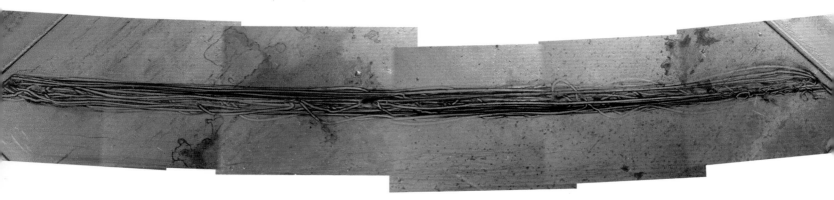

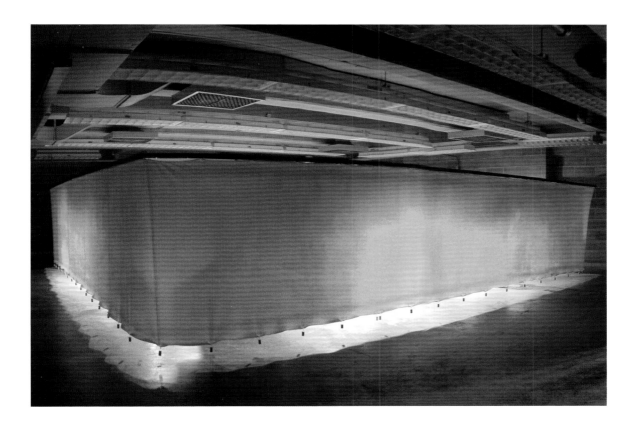

*BEARING (ABOVE),
SCRIBE (BELOW)*

The site for this experiment was an abandoned space in the basement of Wende Hall on the South Campus of the State University of New York at Buffalo. Wende Hall Room 15 is the site where the investigation attempted to reveal the hidden qualities of a space that has seemingly lost its function, its identity, and its meaning. This study resulted in a full-scale, site-specific installation inside Wende 15 that was developed through the careful observations and examinations of the context.

A twenty-foot square steel frame was constructed on the top of four, twenty-four inch square concrete piers that rise fifty inches above the floor. The frame was detailed to move independently from the piers on which it rests. Three of the steel-to-concrete connections are spring-loaded ball casters that allowed the frame to move in the x, y, or z-axis. The fourth was a steel scribe that permanently engraves the movements of the frame into the top of the northern-most pier. A latex skin was draped from the frame in order to make visible the fluctuating movements of the frame. This measuring device is permanently installed to reveal and record the naturally occurring movements of the world that to are invisible to the naked eye.

No two sites on Earth are alike. It seemed appropriate to develop the design scope and scale of the project according to this particular site. Throughout the development of this work there was a constant need to be working on site, to be interacting with site, and to be fully in touch with the immediate surroundings. This investigation hinged on the ability to understand the immediate context of Wende 15 in relation to the distant context of the Earth's motion. It became necessary to accumulate knowledge about the particulars of both the immediate and distant contexts. This led to the acquisition of two types of information. The immediate context was studied by visual observation and analysis of the particulars of the site. The distant context was studied more traditionally, through text based research and interviews with scientists at the National Oceanic and Atmospheric Administration.

DYNAMIC CONCRETE FORM[WORK]
Jose Chang

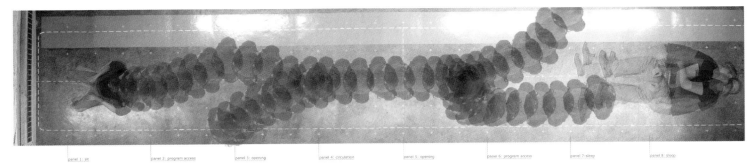

PROGRAM SEQUENCE

CASTING PROCESS

FRANK FANTAUZZI
THESIS CHAIR

BETH TAUKE
THESIS COMMITTEE

PRECEDENTS / SITE

This thesis began with research into the way formwork is traditionally built and a study of the use of flexible materials as concrete formwork. A series of investigations conducted by Mark West using simple pieces of fabric sewn or tied together into formwork were influential in the early process work of this thesis. Another thread of research focused on conventions of concrete casting. More precisely it looked into ways of casting that were dynamic such as tilt-up casting and slip-form concrete. Both methods require site-specific actions even though the formwork used is rigid. Combining ideas from both fields, a new hybrid process of casting was explored.

The site was Wende Hall room 17 and was shared with another student. Once access was granted, the space was divided in half visually using elements in the room such as exposed beams and the window as a divider. Closer examination of the space revealed an overlap in the program, a sliver of space over 3' wide by 26' long between the two spaces. The decision was made to create an intervention in this interstitial space that would physically define the overlap. Since Room 17 was a work space, the overlap would define a shared space used for rest. A program was determined to create space for sleeping, sitting as well as circulation -- reconnecting the two halves of the room.

THE CASTING MACHINE

RECORDING THE BODY

The idea of recording events within the space spawned a series of photographic studies using motioncapture photography methods pioneered by Eadweard Muybridge. These methods were combined with more recent technology such as digital cameras, Photoshop and digital photo stitching that helped record and map how the body began to occupy the interstitial space through the performance of the events. A series of camera mounts were machined and installed throughout the room. Two of the mounts were installed opposite each other to record from front to back. One mount was attached to the side in order to record an elevational view of the space. A fourth mount rode on a rail installed in the ceiling, mapping body motions and events in plan. The rail was required due to the low ceiling and the length of the site. The actions of sleeping, walking and sitting were recorded with a camera and, using Photoshop, were combined into composite images that contained all of the frames.

Questions concerning the form of the cast began to formulate. The first idea was to prescribe the form by examining the composite images and breaking images of the body into a series of points and lines that defined each of the limbs and joints. These movement drawings began to create three dimensional patterns and surfaces that could be translated directly onto fabric formwork and cast in concrete. This method, however, brought up questions concerning representation and the high degree of separation between the body, the event and the cast. In order

FRONT VIEW

to close the gap between body, event and cast, it was decided that a machine would be fabricated to allow the body to directly map its movement through a series of positions in the interstitial space onto the machine. The interstitial space had to be occupied by the body. Each one of the machine's operations was defined by a specific set of actions. This requirement further defined the mechanics and theory behind the machine and the user. The machine was constructed as a hybrid of tilt-up formwork and flexible formwork. It was symmetrical, mimicking the symmetry found in the body and in the space. The entire casting process began with the panels in the vertical position. A series of rods in both panels slid in and out, acting like calipers measuring the passage of the body through the machine. Once this was accomplished,

the rods were mechanically locked into place and the fabric was applied. The panels were then rotated to the horizontal plane to allow the fabric to accept the concrete. The concrete became the recording medium shaping itself around the fabric formwork with the points, physically freezing the movement in time. After a few days of curing, the panels were rotated back to the vertical axis and the concrete was installed into place and released from the formwork. The machine moved along to create the next panel in the sequence and the entire process began again.

ROOM CIRCULATION

PEDESTRIAN AMENITIES + COMMERCIAL DISTRICT REVITALIZATION
Case Study: University Heights Business Community.

Stephanie Simeon

DANIEL B. HESS
THESIS CHAIR
HIROAKI HATA
ALFRED D. PRICE
THESIS COMMITTEE

We are all pedestrians whether we realize it or not. In this automobile driven society a significant portion of the population does not drive. For those that use their feet, a bicycle, or public transit as their preferred mode of transit, the built environment should be an enabler. In a perfect world a pedestrian environment promotes safety and health, local environmental quality, quality of social interactions, and opportunities for recreation and entertainment. It is likely that many local businesses would value such an environment for the health and success of their business.

However, in today's automobile dependent society it is very difficult for business owners to see the benefits of such an environment. In many cases, business owners tend to prefer increased driver amenities over pedestrian amenities because they believe that the majority of their customers arrive in automobiles. Questioning this belief, interviews were conducted to gauge the perception of the University Heights business community. Specifically, there was an interest in determining whether or not a positive link exists between the spatial structures of the pedestrian environment, patronage, and the current revitalization of the University Heights business community.

This research utilized a three-pronged approach: a literature review, street inventory, and community outreach. The literature review revealed an ideal pedestrian environment as an area with human-scale blocks, streets, buildings, parking areas, and signs; buildings close enough to the street and to each other to visually enclose streetscapes; continuous sidewalks with direct connections to building entrances; weather protection via street trees, canopies and other overhangs; flared sidewalks, and other pedestrian crossings aids; and street-level windows.
The second phase of research involved a comparison between the environments noted above to existing conditions within the University Heights commercial

corridor through use of an inventory of pedestrian facilities. The inventory revealed that the University Heights commercial corridor has sidewalks that range in conditions from fair to poor and are not pedestrian friendly. There is a lack of curb cuts; only one was found throughout the entire study area. The lack of curb cuts affects those who use wheeled mobility devices, and strollers, and those who cannot physically access the sidewalk. Poor pedestrian crosswalks prohibit pedestrian refuge. Poor visual continuity of storefronts, which hurts businesses in most commercial corridors. All of these factors, along with others, further enhance auto dependency through the continual neglect of the pedestrian environment.

The third and final phase involved interviewing. There are thirty-nine businesses and institutions within the study area. Using the "on the spot approach" fifteen interviews were completed, one of which was with a major institution. This produced a survey of

thirty-eight percent of the University Height business community. According to business owners a majority of their customers drive, so it was not surprising when sixty percent of them said that providing pedestrian amenities was not important.

Once drivers park to reach a desired location they become pedestrians. With that thought in mind, why are University Heights business owners oblivious to the many benefits of providing pedestrian amenities and encouraging pedestrian travel? A pedestrian-friendly city is good for the economy, and a reduction in car use would free up space for essential business deliveries, benefiting business and customers. With the revitalization along the Main Street corridor, current and future business owners see the positive link between the spatial structures of the pedestrian environment, patronage, and the vitality of the University Heights business corridor.

STEEL PLATE LENSES 4"X 4", 1/8" THICK (FROM LEFT TO RIGHT) APERTURE SIZE: 1/2", 1/4", 1/8", 1/16",1/32"
The larger aperture equals shorter exposure time with a blurred image.
The smaller aperture requires a longer exposure time and produces a sharper image.

TEMPORAL SPACE
Richard J. Maklary

temporal : of or relating to time as distinguished from space : of or relating to the sequence of time or to a particular time.

space : a period of time; also : its duration : a limited extent in one, two, or three dimensions.

MICHAEL ZEBROWSKI
THESIS CHAIR

BETH TAUKE
THESIS COMMITTEE

The human eye is designed to capture images of space around the body and send impulses to the brain where these images are stored in the memory. How do we view the surroundings that we occupy? How does the visual anatomy affect the way content being viewed is processed? How do mediated views affect our understanding of architecture? These questions are relevant to the ways that we design and occupy space.

This thesis proposes a set of methods and systems that capture space through the use of the camera obscura to produce the re-presentation of space. Because of the parameters of the camera obscura, both exterior and interior space were recorded. What was not known at the outset was how the lens size, viewing/distance angles, light intensity, and exposure duration would affect the newly created space.

With the rapid onset of digitization and digitally infused materials, images are increasingly becoming an integral part of built environments. As such, they are affecting the ways that spaces are developed and the ways in which they are perceived. The camera obscura is the first known method of transferring images, and has a rich history that has influenced the way we see. It changed our understanding of the structure of the universe, the ways that space was conceived in art, and the ways that space was represented in architecture. A study of the ways that the camera obscura represents one space in another and, at the same time mediates that space, can help us understand the impact that images can have on the built environment.

The thesis focuses on a process and system that captures views of space with an occupied pinhole camera obscura measuring 5'x 8'x 6'.

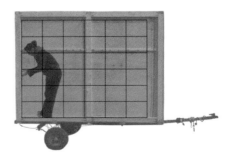

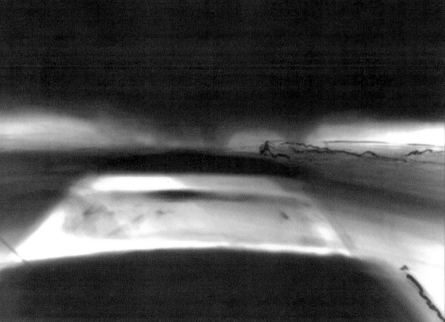

PROCESS

The process designed to capture three chosen spaces was built onto a 5'x 8' flatbed trailer - converting it into a mobile pinhole camera obscura measuring 5'x 8'x 6'. A steel bracket mounted to the front panel of the camera's interior enabled interchangeable lenses of differing apertures. Light entering the camera through these lens projected an inverted, negative image of the exterior onto the interior walls of the camera.

11"x 14" black and white photo paper was installed in the camera's interior (side walls, back wall, ceiling, and floor) using velcro tabs.

- Placing velcro on 150 sheets of paper: 180 min.
- Installing paper in trailer: 75 min.

Once the photo paper was installed, the shutter was opened and the photo paper was exposed to the light. Exposure times varied depending on exterior conditions. After exposure, the paper was removed and stored in light sensitive bags (the operator was inside the camera for the entire process) and transported to a photo lab for developing.

- Exposing paper: 30 min. - 150 min.
- Removing 150 sheets from trailer: 25 min.
- Developing 150 sheets: 540 min.

The process and product using this system allowed the understanding in depth of a given space. The process placed one within the space, hidden from the exterior, able to watch and hear what occurred around the camera. This was possible because, to capture images one had to be inside the camera/trailer during exposures, allowing activity to occur undisturbed. The outcome of this body of work produced a new way of documenting space. The parameters set up made it possible to capture images of a given space through the simple form of pinhole photography, producing images in a manner that more closely resemble the perception of space from the human eye.

As the author of this work I have placed myself into the sense of another world, a feeling of being "inside the outside." The process placed me within the space I had built and also the space that would be documented at the same time, but also disconnected me from my surroundings. Inside the camera/trailer, I was alone in the dark with my thoughts fueled only by what I saw and heard around me through the projection on the interior walls of the camera/trailer. The combination of process and product offered a valuable tool to understanding one's surroundings - an integral factor to design. In this documentation only the product is represented. The process may only be understood through direct experience.

KNOT SCALE 1

KNOT SCALE 2

KNOT SCALE 3

KNOT MAKING
Zhiwei Liao

ANNETTE LECUYER
THESIS CHAIR
OMAR KHAN
THESIS COMMITTEE

This thesis is located at the intersection between digital design and physical fabrication in order to understand the potential and limitations of each of these modes of making, which are central to architectural production. The vehicle for exploration is the elegant proposition of the knot - a three-dimensional entity without beginning or end - which is explored at three 1:1 scales: fabric, the scale of a hand-held object, and the scale of a room. The knot is digitally drawn and manipulated using Rhino software. To control the experiment, it is determined that all physical fabrications should be cast rather than constructed. Materiality is not consistent but rather is calibrated to scale.

The flexible fabric, which is made of interlocking knot modules, is fabricated totally within the digital realm using digital files on a 3-D printer. Made of multiple modules, the fabric is nonetheless a single entity without joints. Each knot is rigid, but the aggregation is flexible as each module is interlocked with, but independent of, other modules.

The hand-held knot straddles the digital and physical realms with a mold made by the 3-D digital printer used for casting hydrocal. The size of the printer governs the size of the mold, requiring the knot to be fabricated using six repetitive segments. This investigation introduces the problem of the joint, which in this mode and scale of fabrication, becomes a weak point both conceptually and literally.

The room-sized knot moves firmly into the physical realm. The digitally generated patterns are now used, not to govern a digital fabrication tool, but to make plywood formwork for reinforced concrete. With this scale and material, the joint is eliminated and the knot can be cast as a single entity. Here resistance is found in the type and thickness of plywood. To achieve the required double curvature, instinct would choose a thin formwork material for flexibility, but instead, empirical evidence from three iterations of formwork lead to the construction of the final form from ¾ inch plywood - scored along digitally determined lines to achieve the required double curvature. The knot must be digitally modified to bring the curvatures within the physical limitations of the plywood.

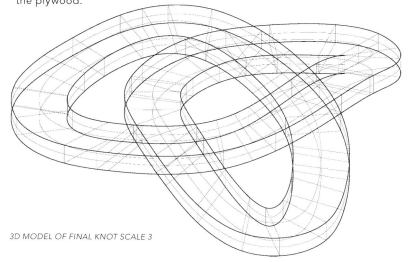

3D MODEL OF FINAL KNOT SCALE 3

  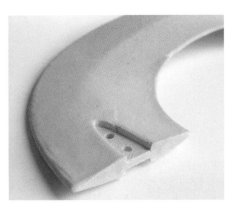 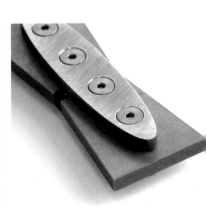

SCALE STUDY MODELS FOR FINAL KNOT

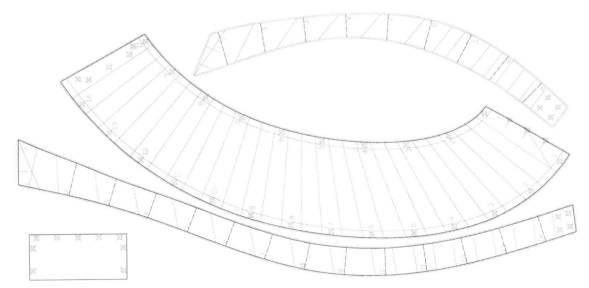

FORMWORK DRAWING

FINAL KNOT

THESIS REVIEW

GRADUATE THESIS . FALL 2005

PO CHI, JIM STERNICK AND BRANDI EUSTICE IN JAPAN

2005 GLOBAL STUDIOS

The Global Studios initiative, developed in 2004, builds upon traditions in the school by offering increased options for summer study abroad, with new programs in Europe and Asia alongside opportunities to participate in an ongoing interdisciplinary studio in Central America. Conducted by architecture faculty, these intensive educational experiences of eight to ten weeks in duration typically include a design studio and two seminars. Supported by a growing number of travel scholarships, both undergraduate and graduate students in the school are encouraged to participate in study abroad programs to gain a broader understanding of architecture and urban planning outside the United States. Many important issues in our disciplines - such as environmental sustainability, social responsibility, the integration of traditional and digital design tools, and how contemporary architecture and urban strategies are integrated in historic contexts – are increasingly matters of both local and global significance. The new perspectives gained by studying and working in other countries give students deeper insights into their own culture and their work in the program.

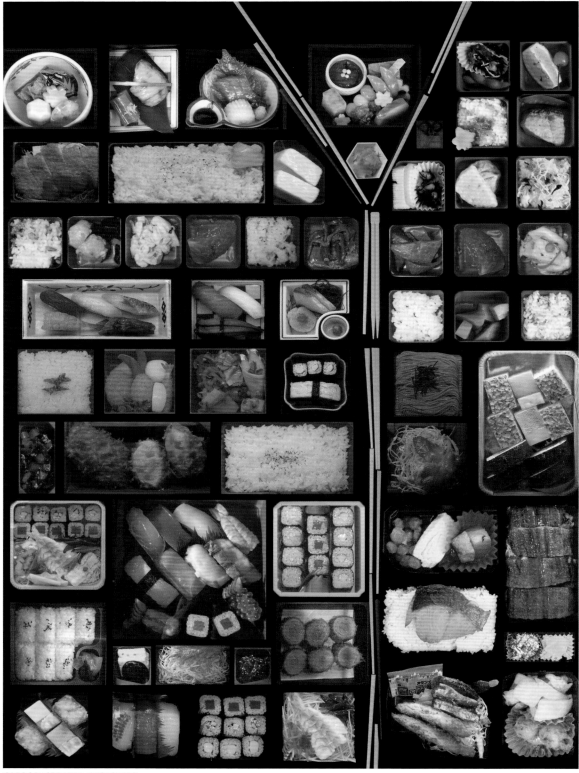

GREGORY SERWETA, KYOTO MAP

JAPAN STUDIO
Sympathetic Imagination

TORBEN BERNS

Seth Amman
Cesar Cedano
Matt Zinski
Gregory Serweta
Joe Carline

A study abroad program is inherently a highly syncretic experience with blurred boundaries defining the structured categories of "educational activities". This experience becomes all the more syncretic in the case of Japan simply by virtue of the radically different context in which both the "familiar" and the "strange" appear.

Rather than produce a vague syncretism in which the student merely brackets "the other" within known quantities of either the overly familiar or the absolutely "unknowable" —and subsequently dehumanized— "exotic", these projects aim to construct a "sympathetic imagination" as a mediating ground. It requires an examination of the student's beginnings and assumptions as much as the implicit ordering of the encountered phenomena.

In line with the overlapping of experience and the nature of the "construction in progress", the work presented here is both collaborative and transgressive. Crossing the techniques and boundaries of disciplines, the projects weave and project to reveal understandings as well as proposals for the "real".

One sequence is comprised of frames extracted from a collaborative effort undertaken as partial fulfillment of the Brush Strokes and Landscape elective. The other sequences are comprised of individual mapping projects of a city.

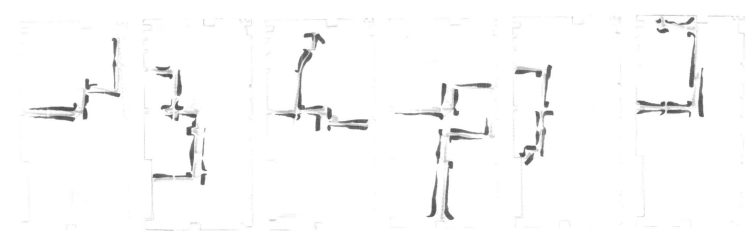

MATT ZINSKI, KYOTO MAP

GARDEN VIDEO; The traditional narrative scroll and both the meditation garden and the strolling garden have evolved concomitantly, weathering changes in both political and religious climates. The affinity between narrative scroll and garden lends itself naturally to the measured structure of video. Each participant proposed a logic for dealing with the traditional garden elements. Each sub-narrative within the video is itself a proposal for a garden, employing the elements of stone, sand, water, waterfalls, bridges, vegetation, walls, paths, and structures. The video is also a

SETH AMMAN
CESAR CEDANO
MATT ZINSKI

The second studio project considered the role of the "personal entertainment/ communication" device. In terms of an architectural manifestation, thought was given to the Shinkenchiku / NTT DoCoMo competition. Discussions highlighted the cultural importance of the 'useless' rather than the 'useful' normally associated with the telephone. Thus the mobile phone as a "recognition device" - one being known by the music content of ones phone and the "peer to peer" network one establishes - is more important than the actual conversations supported by the instrument. This project further inverts this observation by demonstrating the economic potential of the telephone as a tracked "recognition device" as seen from NTT's perspective .

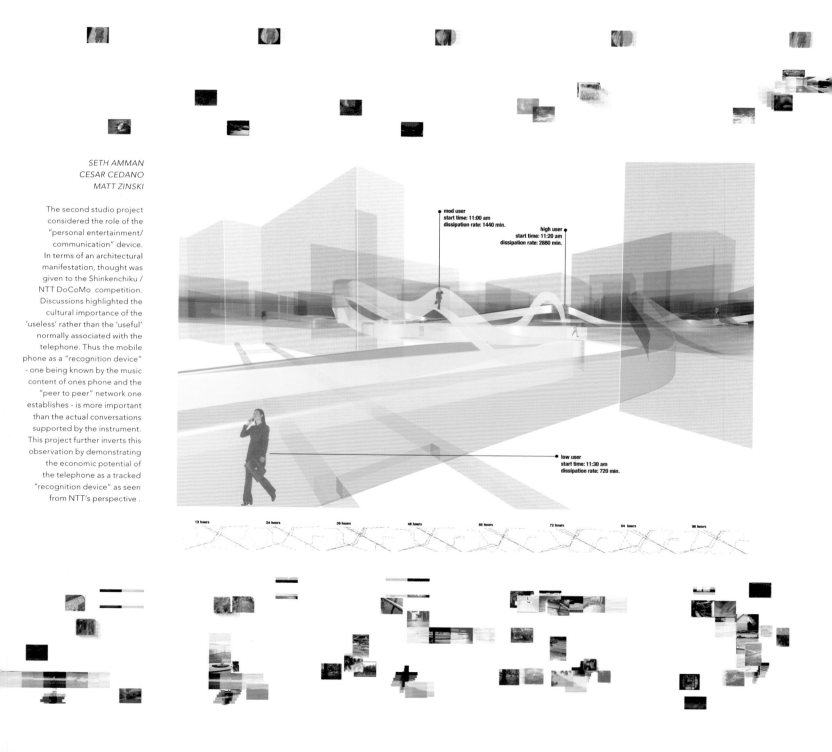

mod user
start time: 11:00 am
dissipation rate: 1440 min.

high user
start time: 11:20 am
dissipation rate: 2880 min.

low user
start time: 11:30 am
dissipation rate: 720 min.

12 hours   24 hours   36 hours   48 hours   60 hours   72 hours   84 hours   96 hours

manifestation of the city where the movement of each individual in mapping his/her garden is bound by both spatial and temporal rules of community. Each frame spills its figurative content into the city authoring a significantly different structure of the city. The rules of inhabitation were as follows: the city was composed of an area of 345600 pixels. Each participant could occupy a maximum of 3600 pixels at any moment with an additional 3600 pixels of ghosted past and anticipated future. Each participant occupied a garden of 1440 frames in a city that spanned approximately 2880 frames in time.

CESAR CEDANO
KYOTO MAP, SHIFTING CITY.

For an occasional visitor to the city of Kyoto, the nature of patterns that appear around the city was striking. Patterns can reshape the city, changing its organization as well as its structure and topography using the following methodology:

- Patterns of varying repetition and color values were sampled from around the city.
- Patterns were organized from left to right.
- A height-field rendered from bitmap using Rhino.
- At rendering time, the patterns organized to create an ascending pattern echoing the topography of the city.
- The blocks of the original city map are broken down to 60 pieces, the same amount of the original pattern map.
- A block's height is determined by relating it to one vertical unit of the pattern's extrusion.

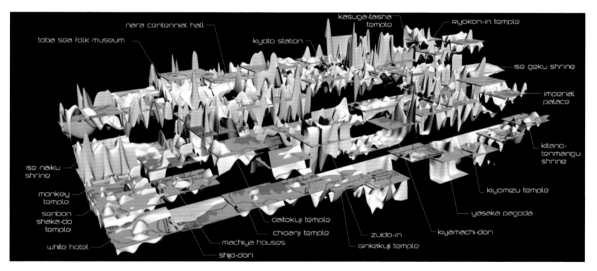

JOE CARLINE
KYOTO MAP, ARTERY.

In response to the axial shift of central Kyoto, an artery of information is explored in detail. Karasuma Dori facilitates the movement of information and matter over time; at once it is static and dynamic. It is concrete, asphalt, stone and brick while embodying human life, conversation and mechanized conveyance. Stripping this artery to reveal its inner workings has entailed "pulling" property line markers from the street surface. The markers represent the most basic organization of the city and their rhythm dictates the flow through this artery.

Through this most basic organizing grid of property lines, the secondary layer of time is explored, exposing the patterns of the city. Night photography is used to look into the flow of information and transition from the Imperial grounds to a new focal point, Kyoto Station. Increasing shutter speed allows more light (information) to be received by the receptors as the viewer's proximity to the center is increased, creating a gradient when viewed at once. Only through the existing grid system can life be experienced, exerting pressure on daily activities along the artery.

JAPAN STUDIO . 2005

COSTA RICA STUDIO
Sustainable Futures/Futuros Sostenible 2005

KEVIN CONNORS

Nathan Alois
Omar Hakeem
James Dankovich
Kim Suczynski

In May 2005, eight UB architecture students set out for Costa Rica. Monteverde, a small pristine area of the tropical cloud forest, was home base for the 10-week summer abroad program.

Students began their studies in the capital city, San Jose, with an introduction to the natural and cultural history of Costa Rica. Visits to the Museo Nacional and Museo Cultural Popular put into perspective the kaleidoscope of ethnic influences current in the young country. The INBio (National Biodiversity Institute) Parque was an opportunity to experience the rare extremes of biodiversity that exist in Costa Rica.

Students then went up the Tilaran Mountains approximately 4,500 feet to the zone of Monteverde and the Monteverde Institute, home to the Sustainable Futures program. The Instituto Monteverde is the de facto planning agency for the political zone. Students became all too familiar with the dirt and stone roads that connected small towns, forest reserves and farm lands in the immediate area, as walking was the primary mode of transportation. But walking was the right pace to take in the spectacular panoramas of the hill country and the exotic species of flora and fauna.

Quakers established the community of Monteverde in 1951 as an experiment in ways of living intended to further peace in the world. For students, Monteverde was the center of a rich mix of Latin American and

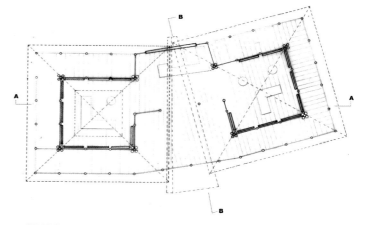

CENTRO DE ARTE; NATHAN ALOIS, OMAR HAKEEM

global cultures, a dynamic landscape formed by still active volcanoes, an environment of lush vegetation, and the setting for incredible displays of native animal behaviors - nesting of the Resplendent Quetzal, the movements of a troop of Capuchin monkeys, or the dawn call of the Bellbirds, just for starters.

The students lived with Costa Rican (Tico) families, studied Spanish three days a week, consumed a diet principally of rice and beans (gallo pinto) and worked on real community projects in an interdisciplinary program with landscape architecture students from Syracuse and Maryland. In the first half of the studio, projects included the development of conservation easements and proposals for levels of access and development at Los Llanos; a public space/facility

South Elevation

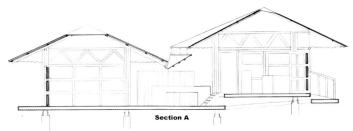

Section A

plan and traffic improvement study for the Village of Santa Elena; and a proposal for new lodging facilities for the Pacific Trail biological corridor.

On breaks, students traveled to a variety of eco-tourist destinations in the cloud forest, to the beaches of the Pacific coast, and to Arenal volcano and its hot springs. Evenings were generally occupied with live music or movies in places like the Lazy Frog or Moon Shiva in Monteverde and usually ended with merengue and salsa dancing in Santa Elena. Games of soccer and ultimate frisbee augmented the physical regime of hiking.

Later in the studio, new community projects were assigned. These included the Enlace Verde Instituto Monteverde – a local conservation easement and long-term development proposal; a design to incorporate the Centro de Arte into the main Institute campus; three scenarios for the upgrading of the Santa Elena Forest Reserve Visitor Center; and a proposed new facility for the Monteverde Conservation League Visitor Center in Cerro Plano. Students worked in teams to inventory local conditions, propose development programs with the local community, study alternatives and present their findings in a public symposium. The projects provided a means of planning for future development and conservation of this precious environment.

While the students left their mark on Costa Rica, the country clearly left its mark on them too. Pura Vida!

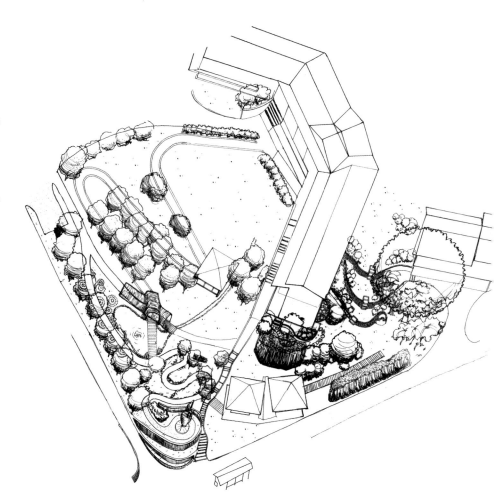

CENTRO DE ARTE; NATHAN ALOIS, OMAR HAKEEM

CENTRO DE ARTE

The Art Center is currently a short distance from the Monteverde Institute (MVI), which owns the property on which the Art Center is presently located. Recently, MVI proposed to relocate the Art Center to the Institute's main campus. With this impending move, several design challenges had to be addressed.

First was the challenge of locating the new Art Center on the Institute campus. The staff of the Art Center stressed the need to be seen from the road because almost all of their business comes from passers-by. This was difficult because the campus is located on top of a hill surrounded by large trees that block any visual connection from the road. This challenge however created the opportunity to give the MVI greater exposure to pedestrians.

The second was the fact that the gallery space would have to fit into an existing bamboo structure that is currently stored in pieces.

The third was finding a place to put a new ceramics studio, a sculptor's space, a photo dark room, and a multi-purpose classroom within the existing campus.

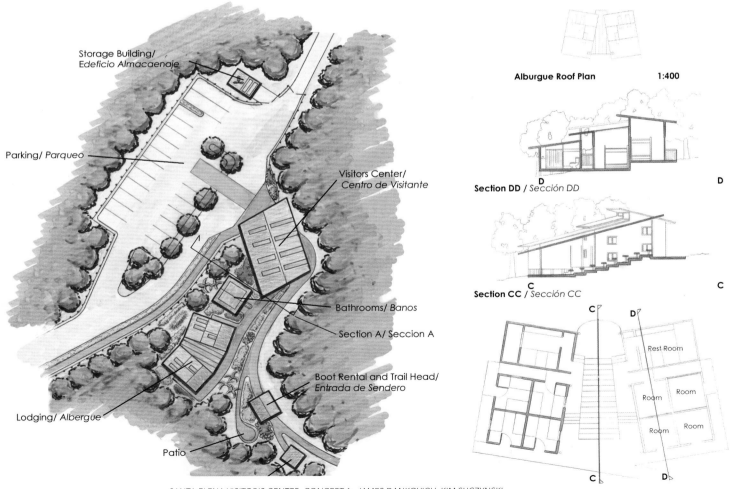

Storage Building/ *Edeficio Almacaenaje*

Parking/ *Parqueo*

Visitors Center/ *Centro de Visitante*

Bathrooms/ *Banos*

Section A/ Seccion A

Boot Rental and Trail Head/ *Entrada de Sendero*

Lodging/ *Albergue*

Patio

Alburgue Roof Plan   1:400

Section DD / *Sección DD*

Section CC / *Sección CC*

Rest Room

Room

Room

Room

Room

SANTA ELENA VISITOR'S CENTER, CONCEPT 1; JAMES DANKOVICH, KIM SUCZYNSKI

The fourth and final challenge would be a way to intertwine the programs of the Institute and the Art Center into a single harmonious balance.

The proposal reconfigures the landscape to create sculpture gardens, water features, pavilions, and access from the road to all of the facilities of the MVI It also includes an addition to an existing studio building. The public bus stop is incorporated into the scheme in order to maximize the new identity of the Art Center/MVI, and improve the environment for travelers, while showcasing new bamboo architecture.

SANTA ELENA RESERVE VISITORS' CENTER

Santa Elena Reserve is a cloud forest preserve on the Pacific slope of the Continental Divide. The reserve has diverse functions in the local ecosystem and community. Leased to the Santa Elena High School by the National Government, the reserve is used as a training facility for tourism and biology students. Students are sent from all over Costa Rica to participate in this unique experience. Over 100,000 people visit the reserve every year.

A visitors' center and facilities for students including housing, a cafeteria, and restrooms were built in 1992. However due to the harsh climate of nearly 100% humidity every day, the complex has become severely damaged due to mold, mildew, and rot, which have compromised the livability and integrity of these buildings.

Three proposals for a new or renovated Visitor's Center and student lodging, including site improvements, were presented to the Director of the Reserve and the Monteverde Institute community.

Parking/ Parqueo

Storage Building/
Almacenaje Edificio

Reception/ Recepcion

Butterfly Garden
/ Jardin de Mariposas

Lodging/ Albergue

Section A/ Seccion A

Bathrooms/ Banos

Visitors Center/
Centro de Visitante

Patio Seating /
Patio

SANTA ELENA VISITOR'S CENTER, CONCEPT 2; JAMES DANKOVICH, KIM SUCZYNSKI

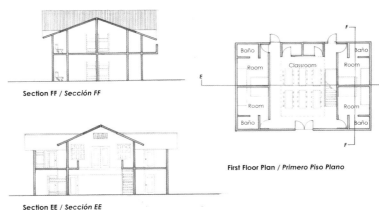

Section FF / Sección FF

Section EE / Sección EE

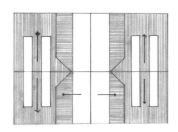

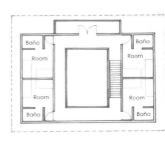

First Floor Plan / Primero Piso Plano

IRELAND STUDIO
Reflections on the Martello Tower

KENNETH MACKAY

Christina Weber
David Goldstein
Ryan Sisti
Lindsay Folger

In *How the Irish Saved Civilization*, Thomas Cahill tells us that texts of the ancient philosophers and early Christian writings were kept from destruction in the monasteries of Ireland. In the isolation of Ireland, an island at the far end of the world, these texts were meticulously transcribed. Cahill's view of history presents us with a poetic image; the process of transcription is a double-edged process of transformation. In transcribing the works of other cultures into their own language, the original works were transformed in the monasteries of Ireland. Conversely, the unique methods used to transcribe generated their own unique cultural history, transforming the Irish culture itself.

Before leaving for Ireland the students received a 5.5" X 8.5" sketchbook in which they were to draw each day while they were in Ireland. However, as opposed to the standard tourist sketchbook which might include picturesque scenes of ruins or townscapes, this sketchbook was to include only architectural details. In preparation for the Summer Studio, the study group met throughout the spring semester and made use of the James Joyce Archive at UB. During this time they reviewed nine readings which included excerpts from Joyce's writing, essays by Seamus Heaney, articles on critical internationalism, and the history of Ireland. In Dublin, the students developed one semester-long project, a visitors' center which would reinterpret Ireland in light of the various readings. The ongoing development of the building design was supplemented by the following four projects.

The first project was a sight analysis of the various Martello Towers, the fortresses built by the British to protect Ireland from a possible Napoleonic invasion. Students explored the various views of the Martello Towers from different points in the city. They were to search for the unexpected framing of the towers from particular locations, consider the orientation and the effects of sunlight on the chosen site throughout the day and return to the site at different times of the day, including sunrise and sunset. The goal of the final product was to capture the unique light of Dublin.

   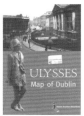  

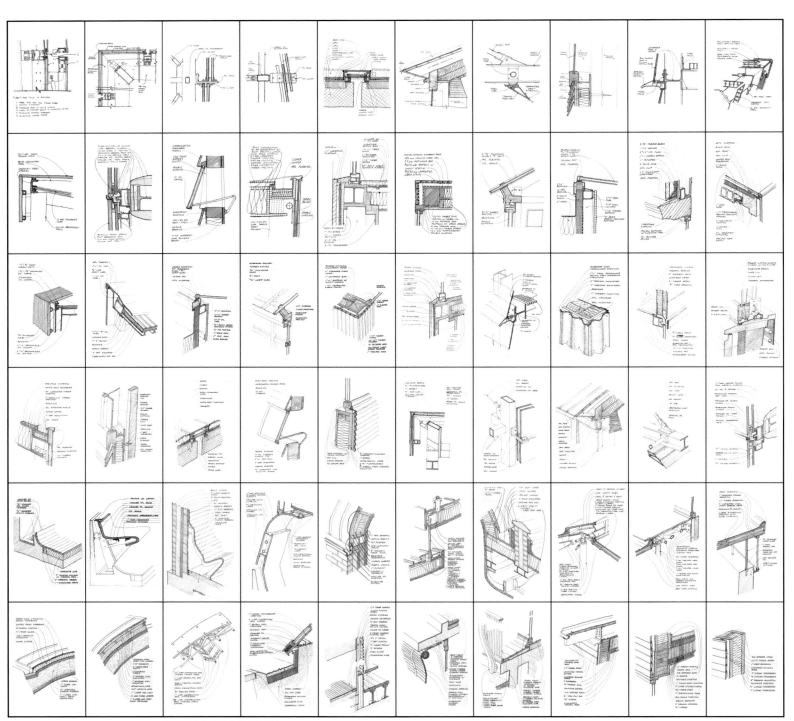

DETAILS, DAVID GOLDSTEIN

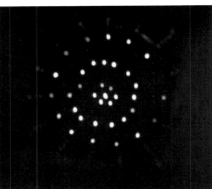

RYAN SISTI

Students chose a site for the second project, and researched various ways in which that portion of the city where the site was located had been documented. The first category of documentation was to include street maps, tourist guides, postcards and images readily available to the tourist. The second category of documentation was to include site plans, infrastructure plans, aerial photos, -- in other words, documentation which is normally available only by interacting with public officials and bureaucrats. Students researched streets and specific sites using the Irish Architectural Foundation.

The third project was an analysis and exploration of the projection of light onto the interior surface of a cylinder. The diameter of the cylinder was required to be large enough to comfortably accommodate the human head. The opening scene of James Joyce's *Ulysses* takes place in a Martello Tower. The cylinders were to be cut into lengths such that the diameter to height ratio was proportional to that of a Martello Tower. Students conducted a series of studies which explored how natural light might be projected onto the interior surface of the tube. They were encouraged to transform the interior surface of the tube and to explore how various apertures which allowed light into the tube might be transformed through translucency, color, images, patterns, etc. The viewer of this model was to be able to place the model over his/her head and control the extraneous light which entered the model. In addition to the model, the final product of this study included a high-resolution image of the interior space.

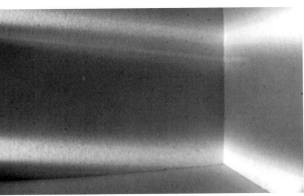

LINDSAY FOLGER

DAVID GOLDSTEIN
Ormond Quay

It was important to consider the location and culture of the surrounding area when designing a program for the site. A public square now resides where the Ormond Market used to stand. The proximity to such cultural markers as the Four Courts, Ormond Hotel, as well as access to the LUAN tram system, make it both a highly accessible and culturally charged site. Consideration was given to the immediate locale as well as other Dubliners.

An earlier lighting study explored the threshold of porosity and security within a cylindrical space. The emphasis of the lighting strategy was to make use of the thickness and malleability of the wall material. A series of baffled edges mediates the incoming light and the city through constricted exterior views. The baffling and an open ground level investigated the application of porosity in design to mediate between public and private space.

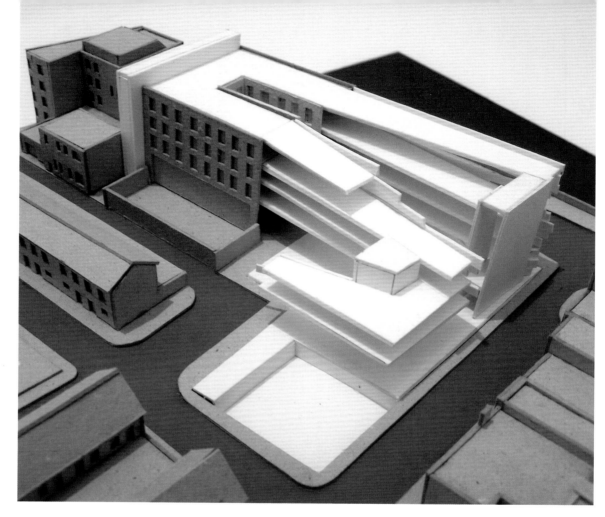

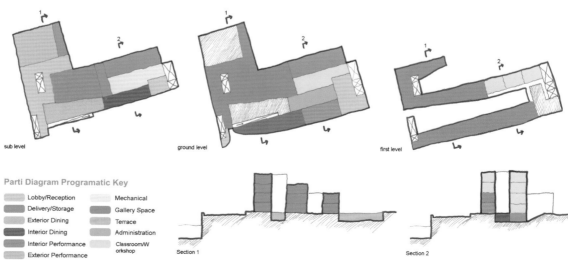

Parti Diagram Programatic Key

Lobby/Reception	Mechanical
Delivery/Storage	Gallery Space
Exterior Dining	Terrace
Interior Dining	Administration
Interior Performance	Classroom/Workshop
Exterior Performance	

sub level

ground level

first level

Section 1

Section 2

DAVID GOLDSTEIN

CHRISTINA WEBER

Walking south on lower Grafton Street I was amazed by a sudden open area with a large triumphal Roman arch opening onto a large public green. To the immediate right was a corner building, not quite the same as its surroundings. Looking as if it wrapped around the corner in a single fluid motion, an interesting effect was created as the southern sun shown across the facade. Its appearance drew me inside where I was awestruck by the light reflecting on the interior walls. These were no ordinary walls – they seemed to be colorful objects floating in a void. A ramp wound around the exterior connecting these objects. The ground floor became a busy gathering space with an information desk, cafe, and large lobby. A large cylinder hovering 10 feet above the floor shot up to the building's roof affording a view to the sky. Punctures through it offered views throughout the rest of the building

CHRISTINA WEBER

RECENT AWARDS
Architecture and Planning

2004 Jay Chatterjee Award for Distinguished Service, ACSP
G. William Page

2004 Chester Rapkin Award, ACSP "Best Article" award
Fare-Free Public Transit at Universities: An Evaluation, the Journal of Planning Education and Research
Daniel B. Hess

2004 First Place, "Designing for the 21st Century" International Competition.
Graduate Student team: Azmi Zahed, Jason Atkins, Natasha Luthra
Faculty Advisors: Beth Tauke, Dennis Andrejko

2005 "Best Student Project," National American Planning Association Award
Food for Growth: A Community Food System Plan for Buffalo's West Side
Fall 2003 Graduate Planning Studio, Samina Raja

2005 "Best Planning Project" National American Planning Association Award
Queen City Hub Plan for Downtown Buffalo
Urban Design Project, Robert Shibley

2005 Symposium Proposal Award, Architectural League of New York
Architecture + Situated Technologies: Responsive Environments, Locative Media, Social Networks
Omar Khan, Mark Shepard

2005 AIA Pilot Project on University Research
A Comprehensive Approach to Teaching Structures Using Advanced Media
Shahin Vassigh

2005 NCARB Grand Prize for "Creative integration of education and practice."
West Side Streetscape Project
Small Built Works Studio + Seminar, Brad Wales

The NCARB Jury commented, "This was a design-build studio series where small projects - unique tangible outcomes - were realized and contributed to the environment of the community. [We] saw an effort to push the limits of design and materials, and the structures were very useful. Students worked with architects, engineers, artisans, contractors, and city officials from design through the permitting process and construction."

2005 NCARB GRAND PRIZE FOR CREATIVE INTEGRATION OF EDUCATION AND PRACTICE.

RECENT AWARDS . 2004-2005

SMALL BUILT WORKS: 2004 - 2006
Performance and Identity Issues

2005 Winner of the NCARB Grand Prize for creative integration of education and practice.

BRAD WALES

Seminar students:
Tim Beebe
Jamie Benz
Ryan Cataldi
Cesar Cedano
Ryan Cole
Nate Cornman
Dane Danielson
Stephen Geltz
Taigo Itadani
Cassie Johnson
Brandon Kline
Andrew Lammon
John Lasher
Chris Potter
Puichee Lee
John Sepples
Sujan Shrestha
Ryan Sisti
Soo Hyun Park
Gilles Van Houcke
Brian Verdone
Emily Wheel
Jon Wolfe
Garrett Wyckoff

The NCARB Award recognized the educational value of constructing small streetscape projects in the city of Buffalo, where students collaborate with community members in all stages of the design-build process. Working directly with local artisans, design professionals, construction trades, and governmental entities, students develop projects from concept to schematic design; from public presentations to the preparation of construction documents for building permits; and then, to fabrication and installation.

The Small Built Works program is fueled by a senior undergraduate option studio offered in the spring term and a construction techniques elective open to both undergraduate and graduate students. Work on six conceptual projects has given rise to four

approved building permits for the construction of twenty-three individual projects in the public domain. The most productive projects include the Community Transformation Project (2001-2004), the Bus Shelter (2002-2005), the Gateway (2003-2005), the Totem (2004-2005), the El Museo (2005-2006), and the Days Park/Wadsworth Project (2006).

Since 2001, 134 students have participated in Small Built Works projects and collaborated with 7 faculty members, 7 licensed architects, 4 engineering firms, 17 local artists, 12 community groups, and 86 individual members of the community. The work has been supported by 32 corporate sponsors and students have worked with 11 different governmental agencies including City Permits, Plan Review,

KLEINHANS MUSIC HALL, DESIGNED BY ELIEL AND EERO SAARINEN, IS THE BACKDROP FOR A NEW BUS SHELTER AT SYMPHONY CIRCLE

Preservation Board, Right-of-Way, Arts Commission, Planning Board, the Councilperson and Mayor's offices, the County Legislator, the County Green Fund, and the Regional Transportation Planning Authority.

Performance and street theater have been integral parts of the Small Built Works pedagogy. The Totem—a rolling rock-n-roll bandstand—literally performs in annual Mardi Gras parades. Projects like the Elmwood-North Kiosk provides a backdrop for changing postings for the Allentown Association community group. Other structures act as places of rest and repose in the city and sites for day-to-day happenings, such as when community members gather together to work on landscaping. As the program has matured, the first round of routine maintenance has

begun and prompted assessments of the performance of construction systems and materials over time in such a demanding climate.

The very public nature of the work—literally on the streets—has brought up issues of identity for both the students and the community. In Buffalo's diverse West Side, students have explored questions of neighborhood imaging in Allentown, Symphony Circle, Connecticut Street, Massachusetts Avenue and the Elmwood Village. In the El Museo Project, the director is seeking to establish a new identity for an existing space. In the Totem Project, students grappled directly with issues of self-identity.

GROUP TOTEM

Students:
Rich Baker
Kevin Brzezinski
Kevin Budin
Dan Clifford
Jason Cosme
Tom Giardina
Eileen Lee
Wendy Lin
John Mandardt
Christopher Mackowiak
Rich Nalepa
John Oldenburg
Joe Scoma
Rob Sikorski
Dave Van Herck
David Goldstein

Bronze Bench:
Pierric DeCoster
Warren Wong

Float reconstruction:
Jake Levine

To'tem, n. [Am. Ind.]
1. among primitive peoples, an animal or natural object considered as being related by blood to a given family or clan and taken as its symbol.
2. an image of this.

And they painted on the grave posts
Each his own ancestral totem,
Each the symbol of his household.

Longfellow.

The Spring 2004 senior studio began with a group totem project in the form of a float for the tenth annual Mardi Gras parade in Buffalo, a sponsored event to benefit Hospice of Buffalo.

Following a design competition within the studio, students voted for the winning proposal, choosing to approach the design of the float in the fashion of the Mardi Gras Indians, not merely as a themed symbol, but as an authentic representation of their community. The result was a rolling rock-n-roll bandstand. One of the students had a band that agreed to play in the streets of Buffalo for Mardi Gras.

Students salvaged two axles from a junkyard to construct a chassis. The float was constructed of structural material donated by a local steel supplier and completed with funding from a second sponsor. A winch-operated scissor truss made the roof semi-retractable for cross-town travel. The rolling bandstand was enclosed on three sides with common plastic sheeting strengthened with batten sleeves and 12-gauge coated wire to stiffen the sheeting. The float was one of thirty entries and won first prize.

INDIVIDUAL TOTEMS

The second half of the studio involved construction of individual totems to be installed in a city-owned vacant lot that was transformed into a sculpture park. After researching the work of David Smith, Alexander Calder, Walter Pichler, Kenneth Anger, Antoni Gaudi, Charles Mackintosh and North American native totems, students were asked to bring in a found object that could form the basis of a personal totem.

The Connecticut Street Business Association provided money for materials and concrete, and students built the formwork, poured foundations, and set steel base plates in early April. The totems were prefabricated in the shop, transported to the site, and welded in place. As with the earlier Bus Shelter Project, students worked with community members on planting and paving.

The City officially took ownership of these structures in the Fall of 2005. Also in the Fall of 2005, two Small Built Works elective students designed a bronze bench for the sculpture park.

EL MUSEO

This project proposes the renovation of a 15' x 65' slot storefront for El Museo, a not-for-profit gallery specializing in Latin American Art. El Museo has been hosting shows of contemporary Spanish-speaking artists for twenty-five years and the gallery has been in it's present location on Allen Street for ten years.

Craig Centrie, the gallery director wanted to make physical improvements. Working with the client, students determined six goals for the project:

- Create a more visually distinctive streetscape.
- Create a donors acknowledgement board near the front of the gallery, visible from the street.
- Provide more wall space and make the gallery space more exciting.
- Increase the efficiency of the office.
- Create visual access between the office and the gallery.
- Create more storage space.

Two constructions are proposed for Fall 2006 to address goals one and two. An exterior canopy, which will require Preservation Board approval, fabricated of steel and translucent panels will create an "outdoor room." A metal silhouette board with interchangeable text capabilities is planned to be suspended on the interior of one of the narrow storefront windows listing major donors. Lighting improvements for the storefront are also planned.

A mezzanine office is proposed to satisfy goals three through six. The new structure will expand the gallery space on the ground floor and admit natural light and through-ventilation from both the street and alley. This will provide a more visually exciting space with more wall surface. It will also open up the possibility of using the alley as an art display and/or performance space. The raised office area will have visual access to the gallery allowing office staff to monitor the gallery space without stopping work.

Construction documents were prepared for a building permit application for the mezzanine in the Fall of 2005; fabrication and installation are in progress during the Spring 2006 term.

El Museo Project:
Ashley Elder
Peter Heller
Christopher Mackowiak

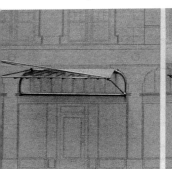
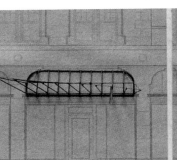
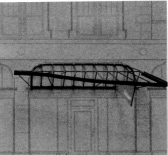
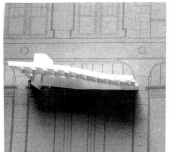

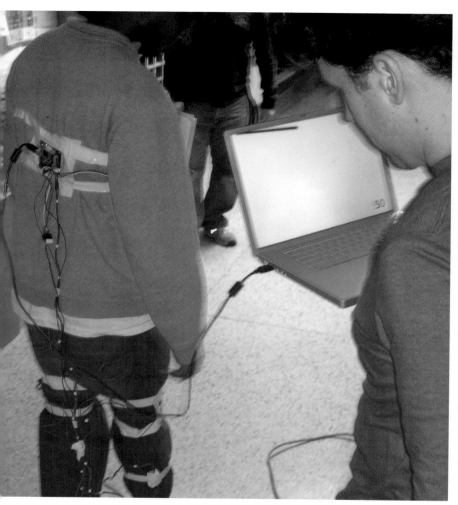
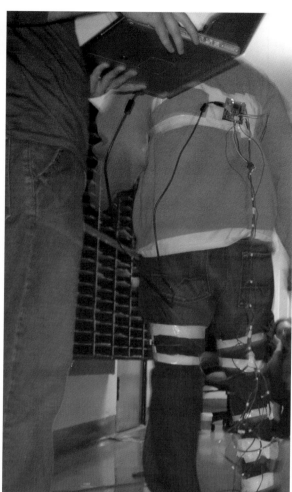

BUFFALO WORKSHOPS

Buffalo Workshops are invested in cutting-edge explorations in technology, design, theory, and pedagogy of architecture. Buffalo Workshops bring designers and specialists of international note to the Department of Architecture to direct workshops that concentrate on contemporary issues of particular significance to the design of buildings and education of architects.

MAKING THINGS
GEHRY TECHNOLOGIES

SENSORS AND ACTUATORS
Making Things . October 2005

Sensors and Actuators was a workshop that introduced students to sensor and actuator technologies for physical computing. The workshop covered electronics concepts and the design of interactive systems. Students learned through lectures and hands-on demonstrations, presentation of related work by media artists and development of interactive projects using Teleo Modules and Flash ActionScript 2.

PARAMETRIC DESIGN
Gehry Technologies . November 2005

The *Parametric Design* workshop introducing parametric and associative geometry in Computer Aided Design. The workshop utilized Gehry Technologies' CATIA based Digital Project to demonstrate how to design and build relational geometries. Students learned how to develop models with persistent geometric relationships that can be altered and updated through parametric and dimensional changes.

"I was moved by these buildings, and that was partly because I came upon them unprepared. They were as unknown to me as they must be to any student or lover of architecture because, outside the modernists' polemics of the twenties, they have practically no part in the records of architectural history..."

Reyner Banham, A Concrete Atlantis

THE PETER REYNER BANHAM FELLOWSHIP

Peter Reyner Banham [SUNY Buffalo 1976-1980] produced a foundational body of scholarship on material and visual culture as a reflection of contemporary social life. The Banham Fellowship in Architecture at Buffalo supports design work that situates architecture within the general field of socio-cultural and material critique.

PETER REYNER BANHAM

HILARY SAMPLE
2004-2005 BANHAM FELLOW

Hilary Sample taught a graduate design studio in which students proposed designs for a National Science Foundation ERE Tower in San Francisco and researched reflexive infrastructures in the seminar *21st Century Urban Infrastructures*. Her exhibition *Ambient Technologies*, presented work from the studio and also a 1:1 scale facade mock up that examined methods for registering the environment of its interior and exterior surroundings at the site of the building skin. This research is part of the project *Sensing Facades*. As an architect, teacher and writer, Hilary Sample's work focuses on the relationships between architecture, environment and technology. Issues of maintenance in architecture studied at different scales including the design of sensing facades, building systems and healthy urbanisms are the focus of her forthcoming book *SICK CITY - infrastructures, urbanisms and diseases in the 21st century city.*

JONATHAN SOLOMON
2005-2006 BANHAM FELLOW

Jonathan Solomon's work explores the consequences of making planning complicit with unstructured organizational principles at a range of scales: from applying post-Fordist production techniques to structural grids, to studying the free-market economy as a generating force for urban planning. His design proposals for a flexibly specific transportation landscape were published in 2004 as *Pamphlet Architecture #26. 13 Projects for the Sheridan Expressway*. Solomon is a founding editor of *306090 Architecture Journal*. His work with students in his seminar and studio was presented in the spring 2006 exhibition entitled *Markestructures: Case studies in and design proposals for the privatization of urban infrastructures*. His work presented here centers on a technics seminar offered in the Fall 2005 term investigating issues of flexible specification.

HUI KIM

NATIONAL SCIENCE FOUNDATION ERE TOWER
San Franciso

HILARY SAMPLE
04-05 BANHAM FELLOW

Lindsay Bishop
Melissa Hidalgo
So Hui Kim
Jeff Kloetzer
Min Li
Peter Mendola
Derek Morgan
Dirk Pfeifer
Dan Puff
Keegan Roberts
Marc Rodriquez
Qi Wang
Yuzhu Zheng

Architecture today holds the promise of sensing its environment through ambient technologies. These types of technologies respond to environment rendering architecture as background. Environment can have a multitude of meanings - micro or macro climate, weather, wind, light, fog and instability of ground (earthquakes, etc). Concepts such as visible vs. invisible, climatic conditions vs. controlled conditions, and patterns become the premise for incorporating technology and environment as a strategy for designing alternative models of the tower.

This studio project examined the intersection of architecture and environment as the problem for the design of the new headquarters for the National Science Foundation Environmental Research and Education Building, a tower in downtown San Francisco. The goal of the studio was to investigate building skins and their use as an environmental interface. The project was a twofold investigation beginning with the first half of the term examining at specific problems of building skins and the second further developing one of the proposals into full a facade for a tower. As part of the tower proposal, the program fuses institutional categories of research, office, archive/library and interactive spaces for the public as a new typology.

DIRK PFEIFER

After a field trip to New York visiting offices of SOM and KPF and the Skyscraper Museum the students produced a series of large scale models from facade details to models of their towers at a larger scale. The projects varied in emphasis but all explored ideas of environment, facades and public spaces. So Hui Kim's elegant twisting tower sublimely grows around a shifting courtyard, that extends the entire height of the tower to provide light and air to otherwise dark offices and research labs. Yuzhu Zheng's shimmering tower exploited the play between public and private, keeping program for each separate on either side of an internal open atrium with projecting balconies that become viewing platforms and impromptu meeting areas. Marc Rodriquez, coded tower of fluctuating transparencies and colors organized a matrix of spatial and programmatic overlaps. Other projects interpreted the public access as new means of circulation. Peter Mendola's endless spiraling stair and ramp giving 24 hour access to the building, Min Li's wrapping stair and platforms explored issues of thickness in structure and skin. Others developed systems of enclosure based on loose skins with diaphanous qualities. Lindsay Bishop's weaving facade, Melissa Hidalgo's thick facade, Dan Puff's inflating translucent facades and Keegan Roberts curtain of compressible circles investigated systems of environmental response as movable skins. Dirk Pfeifer's preoccupation with qualities of osmosis and elasticity literally grew the building across the site; layering rather than taking it upwards challenged the notion of economy and public access. Others focused on performance spaces. Derek Morgan, Jeff Kloetzer and Qi Wang's exploration of the exchange between public and private resulted in interlocking spaces planned around site issues of light, wind and noise, testing traditional ideas of towers.

JEFF KLOETZER

YUZHU ZHENG

QI WANG

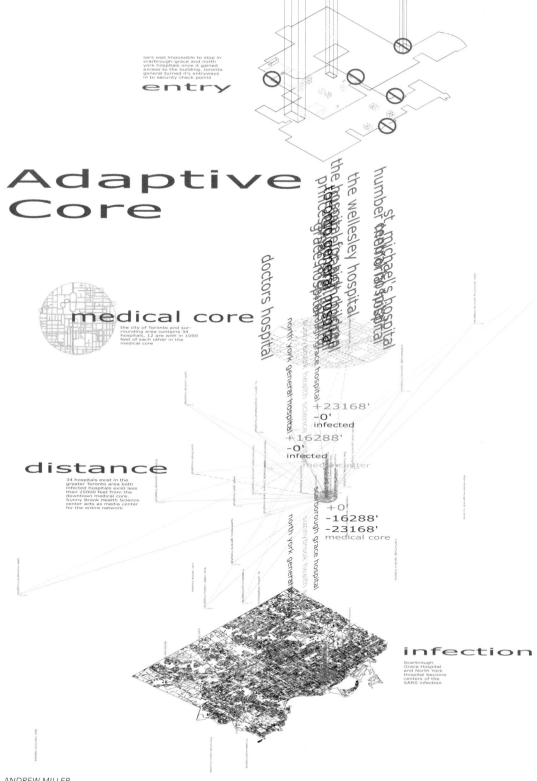

sars was impossible to stop in
scarbrough-grace and north
york hospitals once it gained
axcess to the building. toronto
general turned it's entryways
in to security check points

entry

Adaptive
Core

medical core

the city of Toronto and surrounding area contains 34
hospitals, 12 are with in 1000
feet of each other in the
medical core

doctors hospital

the wellesley hospital

humber regional hospital

st. michael's hospital

the toronto general hospital

princess grace hospital

north york general hospital

sunnybrook health science

scarborough grace hospital

+23168'
-0'
infected

+16288'
-0'
infected

media center

distance

34 hospitals exist in the
greater Toronto area both
infected hospitals exist less
than 25000 feet from the
downtown medical core.
Sunny Brook Health Science
center acts as media center
for the entire network

+0'
-16288'
-23168'
medical core

north york general

sunnybrook health

scarbrough grace hospital

infection

Scarbrough
Grace Hospital
and North York
Hospital become
centers of the
SARS infection

ANDREW MILLER

21ST CENTURY INFRASTRUCTURES

HILARY SAMPLE
04-05 BANHAM FELLOW

Alexandra Rabuffo
Andrew Miller
Brandi Eustis
Jennifer Oakley
Loi Tran

This seminar prompted each student to examine conditions of reflexive infrastructures found in contemporary cities. As a research seminar, this project helped students understand the complexity of issues surrounding infrastructures and their relationships to architecture and urbanism. Infrastructures enable integration of new developments or expansion of pre-existing conditions within global, national or local networks. Infrastructures act as information distribution networks with specific modes for interfacing with the public. Operating within the public realm, how do infrastructures evolve in the expansion and maintenance of cities in response to new developments?

The students identified new types of infrastructures dealing with emergencies in the city. The students focused on the events of SARS and the cities that it impacted from Beijing, Taipei and Hanoi to Toronto. They worked independently and produced original drawings and maps about a city of their choice. Researching a particular theme or situation enabled them to learn about each city's organization of public health and transit infrastructures. The projects evolved to produce new maps of each city, some identifying infrastructures used for just one day versus a more complex system affected over a course of weeks, such as Alexandra Rabaffo's three dimensional stratified map of Beijing. Andrew Miller examined Toronto's hospital system from the urban scale down to the corridor of Toronto General Hospital. Similarly Brandi Eustis identified the hospitals affected by SARS and mapped the location of each hospital comparing its urban context and public spaces. Jennifer Oakley explored temporary aid infrastructures employed in Banda Aceh and Sumatra after the South East Asian Tsunami. These studies focused on the urbanization of disease and its impact on infrastructures. In crisis, these systems provide the potential for spontaneous response, avoiding breakdown and further economic disaster.

CARE, CCF, CWS, DAI, IFRC, IRC/IOM, IRD, IMC, INDONESION RED CROSS, JHPIEGO, MECRCY CORPS, PCI, SC/US, WHO, WVI, USAID INDONESIA, UNHCR

JENNIFER OAKLEY

JENNIFER OAKLEY

LOI TRAN

ROADWAY OVERPASSES +60'
SUBWAY TUNNELS -20'

TRAIN ACCESS LINES +20'

ALEXANDRA RABAFFO

THEORY AND APPLICATION OF FLEXIBLE SPECIFICATION

JONATHAN SOLOMON
05-06 BANHAM FELLOW

Stalin Duran
Timothy William Hoskins
Kang Yau Lee
Lisi Li
Christopher M. Mackowiak
Michael Nowak

During the 20th Century, the Modernist design aesthetic developed in tandem with the growing force of mass production and theories of top-down social organization. While this paradigm has been critically re-evaluated since it came into existence, its constituent elements—what a building looks like, what it means, and how it is made—have only been addressed individually: the synthetic model has yet to be matched. Meanwhile, mass production, though it remains a powerful force in the building trades, has elsewhere all but given way to mass customization. Recent advances in computer aided design technologies, breakthroughs in conceptual models of systems convergence, and innovations in numerical fabrication technology (here compiled under the heading Flexible Specification)* have created the potential to revolutionize the way architecture is imagined and built. This course engaged these technologies, tools and conceptual models not simply by employing them singly, but by conceptualizing them in an integrated way.

Organized as a seminar, this course functioned more like a workshop or laboratory in techniques of Flexible Specification: the mass-customization of repeated elements; autonomous integration of structure, space and program and the development of emergent systems out of a flexible generic typology.

MICHAEL NOWAK, FINAL RENDERING

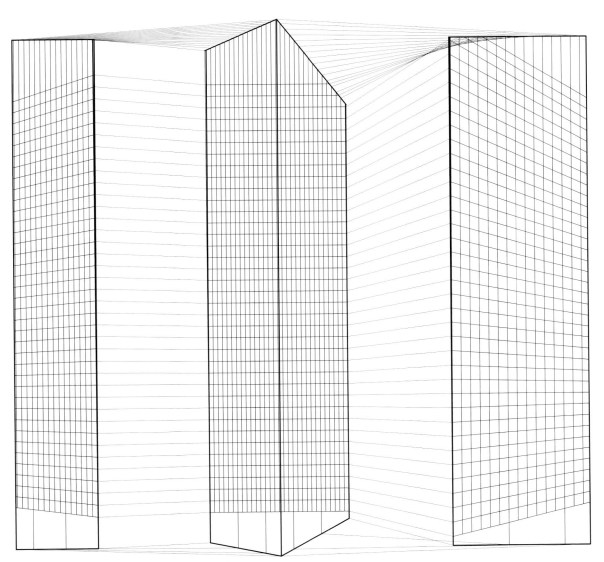

MICHAEL NOWAK, PERSPECTIVAL FACADE ALTERATION

MICHAEL NOWAK
The Flexible Icon

This project challenges the iconic image of the Seagram Building as photographed by Ezra Stoller, exploring the conflict between the agenda of the architect and the agenda of the photographer. The altered building forces a point of view visible from only one location, an application of the orthogonal, elevational window grid on the forced perspective view presented by Stoller. The result is a building façade that becomes, paradoxically, less orthogonal.

Stoller's photograph was scanned and imported into AutoCAD. A CAD drawing was made of the flattened elevations. This grid was then placed over the Stoller photo. The grid was scaled so that the flat planar West façade matched the width of the tower in Stoller's photo with a new grid that was no longer orthogonal.

The newly manipulated grid was imported into Rhinoceros, 3D NURBS modeling software, in order to produce a three-dimensional model of the entire tower. A series of perspective view renderings was then made, each from a different point of view at the same height of Stoller's photograph. As the renderings illustrate, the idealized Mies grid can only be found at one specific point of view, the chosen view of Stoller. Only at this one specific point in space can Mies' original vision presented in his sketch be found on the facades. As soon as the observer moves the perspective foreshortening of his grid becomes more severe than Stoller could have ever created with a wide-angle lens.

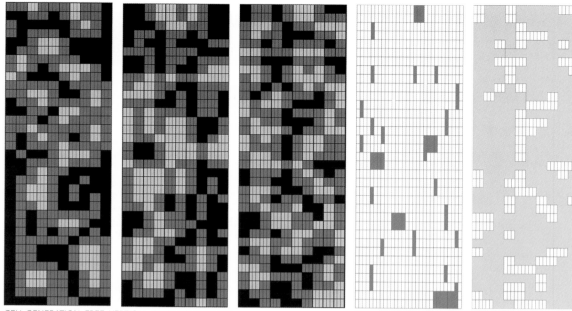

CELL GENERATION; FREE, VERTICAL, EVEN DISTRIBUTION

CONNECTIONS; TRANSVERABLE, VISUAL OR ACCOUSTIC

LISI LI
Reorganizing the Seagram

This project proposes a bottom-up transformation of the Seagram Building in appearance, organization and circulation. By acting minimally on a simple element in the structure, changing the length of the connection member that attaches the curtain wall to the floor slab, a rippled curtain wall with openings accommodates various connection modules between floors. The new design was processed through an algorithm to maximize flat glass panels, simplifying the production module without altering the organizational module. The remaining triangulated panels become opaque metal cladding.

In his book *Emergence,* Steven Johnson illustrates how bottom-up design concepts produce global results from collective local actions. This approach emphasizes the behavior of individual design modules, and relationships between these modules. For example, new connection will encourage information exchange. The behaviors of these connection modules directly affect the functional programs behind them and the larger organization of the building around those programs. In this case, six one-storey cell grids are defined and different rule sets applied to them: First, no more then three cells can be connected vertically or horizontally. Second, all cells that represent traversal and acoustic connection modules can only connect to like cells, Third, all acoustic connection cells can connect to all types of cells. Lastly, all null connection cells can only connect to like and acoustic cells.

MAXIMIZED PANAL FACADE (ABOVE), FINAL COLLAGE (RIGHT)

Students utilized the computer as a design tool (Autodesk, Rhinoceros, or equivalents and the school's digital workshop) as well as hand modeling in pursuit of a directed design project. Multiple iterations or prototypes were produced, testing the theory and application of Flexible Specification in architecture at a range of scales. The development of these projects comprised the primary material of the course.

The seminar began with a comparative analysis of two historical precedents in the deployment of the module: the work of Modernist Mies van der Rohe and Metabolist Kisho Kurokawa. Specifically, Mies's work was examined through a specific structural system, the curtain wall, which flourished and thrived under the rubric of mass production and was integral to the aesthetic and conceptual project which situated mass production alongside homogenizing forces of minimalism and universal space.

The course unfolded around a series of critical re-approaches (not re-appropriations, and not reproaches) to these projects, and by extension to architecture at large, under the rubric of mass customization. These new approaches were structured as experiments worked through in models and drawings and informed by a series of readings and discussions. They address, through design proposals, the question of what becomes possible when mass-produced identical modules at every scale (from the detail, to the structural element, to the spatial unit, to the building itself) are replaced by mass-customized modules that vary.

*The term "Flexible Specification" refers specifically to the architectural applications of an economic term, "Flexible Specialization" (see: Amin, Ash, ed. Post-Fordism, a Reader. Oxford: Blackwell, 1994). As such, it draws on analogs in economics, manufacturing, structures and philosophy, but occupies specifically the arena of architectural expression.

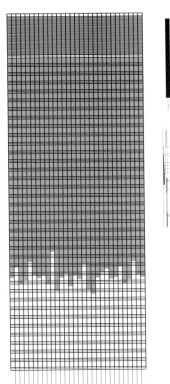

VETO CONFIGURATION

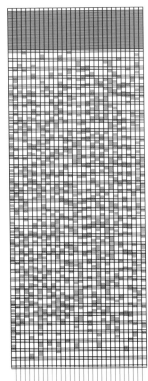

FULL PIXEL CONFIGURATION

CHRISTOPHER MACKOWIAK
Seagram Skyline

The Seagram Building is defined as much by light as it is by structure: during the day, it appears as an opaque obsidian shard pointing to the sky, while by night it becomes transparent and radiant. Mies van der Rohe, in an effort to control the purity of these effects, designed window shades for the Seagram building which would be operable in only two conditions: open and closed. The client of course preferred a flexible system. A compromise was made to design a window shade operable in three positions; open, half-open, and closed.

The Seagram building is also one of the most significant curtain wall skyscrapers in America. The construction methods yielded a cavity between the edge of the floor slab and the glass. It is in this space that I propose an altered sunshade system. A series of single, 40-storey window shades replaces the many smaller, individual window shades, altering the street presence of the building in a variety of ways.

The application of this system to the Seagram façade could lead to the reorganization of the building's program, with greater respect to the section. Businesses would no longer rent a floor; rather offices would occupy the vertical slices which they control. Another implication could be more nuanced control over the building's street presence. The Seagram building no longer behaves simply as a glowing skyscraper in the dark: The shades can reduce the visible building height, thus dramatically changing the New York City skyline.

THE JOHN AND MAGDA MCHALE FELLOWSHIP

Magda Cordell McHale and John McHale, who both taught at SUNY, were among the founders of the Independent Group, the British movement that grew out of a fascination with American mass culture and post-WWII technologies. The McHale Fellowship supports design work that involves speculation on the impact of new technologies on architecture.

MAGDA CORDELL MCHALE

JAMES CATHCART
2005-2006 MCHALE FELLOW

A graduate of the Cranbrook Academy of Art, James Cathcart has worked in proctice with Ralph Applebaum Associates in New York. His independent collaborative work is documented in *GRAVITY*, Pamphlet Architecture #25. Cathcart, a New York based architect, was in residence at the University at Buffalo School of Architecture and Planning during the Fall 2005 semester, where he taught an upper level graduate studio (right), presented a lecture of his work, and directed a collaborative installation in the Dyett Gallery.

CATHCART GRADUATE STUDIO FINAL REVIEW

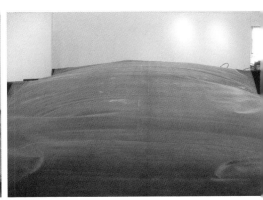

2005 MCHALE FELLOWSHIP EXHIBITION
BODY BAG
James Cathcart with Frank Fantauzzi and Dan Gallagher

March 20, 2003:   America launches first series of air strikes on Bagdad, described by the military as the "Decapitation Attack"

March 21, 2003:   Beginning of operation "Shock and Awe"

May 1, 2003:   President Bush addresses the nation from aboard the USS Abraham Lincoln on May 1, with a banner in the background announcing "Mission Accomplished"

October 22, 2003:   The Washington Post reports that the Bush administration had ordered the Pentagon to prevent any news coverage of the bodies of US troops being sent home from Iraq.

October 26, 2005:   American military casualties reach 2000.

The project's mission was to visualize the volume occupied by 2000 bodies with an average volume of 2.80 ft^3 per body. The volume is contained by a rubber membrane (EPDM), typically used in the roofing industry. Two sheets of this rubber were seamed at the edges and inflated to the required volume capacity using compressed air.

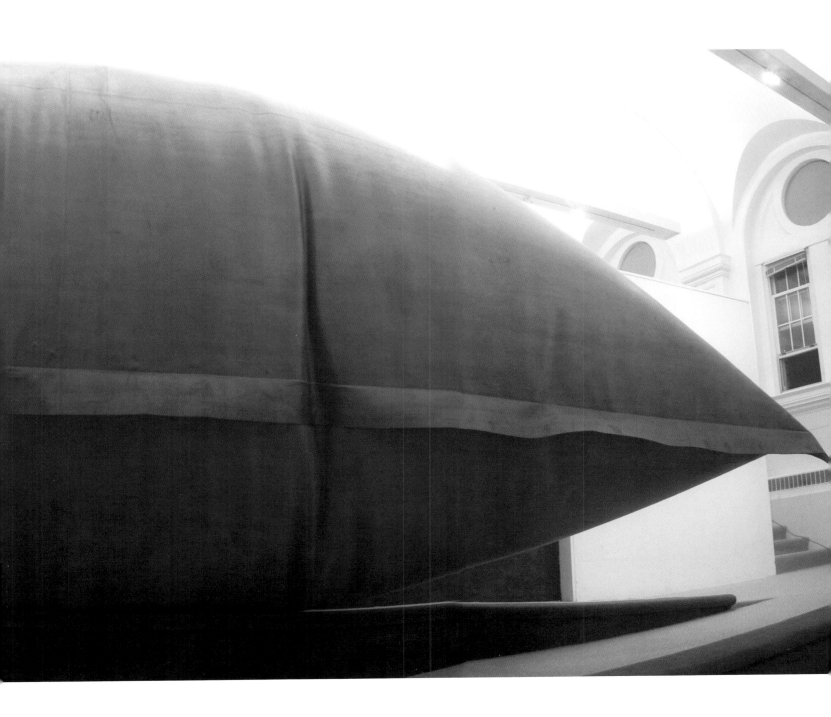

PETER DREIER

THE CLARKSON VISITING CHAIRS IN ARCHITECTURE AND PLANNING

Peter Dreier, Spring 2005 Clarkson Chair in Planning

The Clarkson Chair endowment was established in 1990 by Will and Nan Clarkson to bring a senior visiting professional or scholar in a relevant area of study within the school's mission to Buffalo to spend a week in residence, be available to students and faculty, give a public lecture, and present seminars in their specific areas of expertise. The first recipient of the Clarkson Chair visited the school in 1990. Since 2000, the Clarksons have been supporting two scholars each year, one in Architecture and one in Planning.

WILL AND NAN CLARKSON

Professor Dreier, the Dr. E.P. Clapp Distinguished Professor of Politics and Director of the Urban and Environmental Policy Program at Occidental College in Los Angeles, has been an active force in the development of community planning and has written extensively about the intersection of physical planning, urban policy and the communities that planning is organized to serve. He is joint author of *Boston's West End 35 years after the bulldozer* and *Regions that work: How cities and suburbs can grow together.* The most recent book that he co-authored, *Metropolitics for the Twenty-first Century,* draws attention to the dilemmas and potentials of urban and suburban growth. Peter Dreier also served as a senior policy advisor to Ray Flynn, the Mayor of Boston, from 1984 to 1992 before moving to the west coast. It was this unique combination of academic research, community involvement and professional experience that made him such an excellent appointment as the 2005 Clarkson Chair in Planning.

While in Buffalo, Peter worked closely with students in a number of classes including PD 460 Visions of the City, PD 508 Race, Class, Gender and the City, and PD 525 Financing Urban Development. His opening colloquium, an urban development forum with guest panelists from HUD, the State of New York, and the Federal Reserve Bank, was titled "Emerging Trends in Urban Policy and Impacts on Planning Practice." He participated in a series of workshops with community leaders that were organized by the UB faculty. In these sessions he spoke about his own experiences in Boston and Los Angeles and was actively engaged in discussions about developments in Buffalo.

In a public lecture Dreier highlighted aspects of his own work and sought to locate those experiences in the context of Western New York. His comments regarding the inner city and the potential and realities of urban and community planning were provocative and enlightening.

2005 Glenn Murcutt
2004 Peter Zumthor
2004 Michael Kwartler
2003 Lars Lerup
2003 Gerrit-Jan Knaap
2001 Alan Artibise
2000 Mark Wigley
2000 Michael Storper
1999 K. Michael Hayes
1998 Robert Yaro
1996 Sanford Kwinter
1995 Patsy Healey
1994 Daniel Hoffman
1993 M. Christine Boyer
1992 Alberto Perez-Gomez
1991 John Forester
1990 Marco Frascari

DENNIS SHELDEN

EINAR JARMUND

LYNNE SAGALYN

JOSHUA RAMUS

THOM MAYNE

KEVIN DALY

PETER DREIER

STEVEN HOLL

S H E L D E N
JARMUND VIGSNÆS
S A G A L Y N
R A M U S @ O M A
M A Y N E
DALY GENIK
D R E I E R
H O L L
S Z E T O
B A I R D
A D J A Y E

GEORGE BAIRD

DAVID ADJAYE

Dennis
SHELDEN
Einar + Hakön
JARMUND VIGSNÆS
Lynne
SAGALYN
Joshua
RAMUS@OMA
Thom
MAYNE
Kevin Chris
DALY GENIK
Peter
DREIER
Steven
HOLL
Yvonne
SZETO
George
BAIRD
David
ADJAYE
Tsurumaki Lewis
LEWIS
Beatriz
COLOMINA
David
ORR
Julie
BARGMANN
Greg Pasquarelli
SHoP
Caruso
ST.JOHN
James
CATHCART
Jian
ZHOU
Sauerbruch
HUTTON

DAVID LEWIS
BEATRIZ COLOMINA

LEWIS
COLOMINA
ORR
BARGMANN
SHoP
ST.JOHN
CATHCART
ZHOU
HUTTON

DAVID ORR

GREG PASQUARELLI

PETER ST.JOHN

JAMES CATHCART
LOUISA HUTTON

Dennis
SHELDEN
Einar + Hakön
JARMUND VIGSNÆS
Lynne
SAGALYN
Joshua
RAMUS@OMA
Thom
MAYNE
Kevin Chris
DALY GENIK
Peter
DREIER
Steven
HOLL
Yvonne
SZETO
George
BAIRD
David
ADJAYE
Tsurumaki Lewis
LEWIS
Beatriz
COLOMINA
David
ORR
Julie
BARGMANN
Greg Pasquarelli
SHoP
Caruso
ST.JOHN
James
CATHCART
Jian
ZHOU
Sauerbruch
HUTTON

BUFFALO BOOKS

SCHOOL OF ARCHITECTURE AND PLANNING
University at Buffalo
The State University of New York
Hayes Hall
3435 Main Street
Buffalo, New York 14214-3087

www.ap.buffalo.edu

EDITORIAL BOARD
Editor: William C. Helm II
Design: William C. Helm II, Michele Han, Tsui Ying Ip (Jade), Clare Smith
Advisors: Dean Brian Carter, Sam Cole, Omar Khan, Jean La Marche, Annette LeCuyer, Jonathan Solomon
Consultants: Ruth Bryant, William McDonnell, Cheryl O'Donnell, Barbara Patolli
Printing: Digicon Imaging, Inc.
Printed and bound in the United States of America
Typeset in Avenir, designed by Adrian Frutiger

Additional copies and back issues are available at the above address or by visiting the *Intersight* web site:
http://www.ap.buffalo.edu/intersight

9 | First Edition
Cataloging-in-Publication Data
Intersight volume 9 / William C. Helm II, editor
ISBN 0-9707863-9-5
ISSN 1049-6564